Origami Symphony No. 11

Folding on Land, Air and Sea

Books by John Montroll
www.johnmontroll.com
Instagram: @montrollorigami

Origami Symphonies

Origami Symphony No. 1: The Elephant's Trumpet Call
Origami Symphony No. 2: Trio of Sharks & Playful Prehistoric Mammals
Origami Symphony No. 3: Duet of Majestic Dragons & Dinosaurs
Origami Symphony No. 4: Capturing Vibrant Coral Reef Fish
Origami Symphony No. 5: Woodwinds, Horns, and a Moose
Origami Symphony No. 6: Striped Snakes Changing Scales
Origami Symphony No. 7: Musical Monkeys
Origami Symphony No. 8: An Octet of Cats
Origami Symphony No. 9: Ode to Australia
Origami Symphony No. 10: Lucky & Dangerous Sides of Origami
Origami Symphony No. 11: Folding on Land, Air and Sea

Animal Origami

Arctic Animals in Origami
Origami Aquarium
Dogs in Origami
Perfect Pets Origami
Dragons and Other Fantastic Creatures in Origami
Bugs in Origami
Horses in Origami: Second Edition
Origami Birds: Second Edition
Origami Gone Wild
Dinosaur Origami
Origami Dinosaurs for Beginners
Prehistoric Origami: Dinosaurs and other Creatures: Third Edition
Mythological Creatures and the Chinese Zodiac Origami
Origami Sea Life: Third Edition
Bringing Origami to Life: Second Edition
Origami Sculptures: Fourth Edition
African Animals in Origami: Third Edition
North American Animals in Origami: Third Edition
Origami for the Enthusiast: Second Edition
Animal Origami for the Enthusiast: Second Edition

Geometric Origami

The Magic of Origami Polyhedra
Origami Stars: Second Edition
Galaxy of Origami Stars: Second Edition
Origami and Math: Simple to Complex: Second Edition
Origami & Geometry
3D Origami Platonic Solids & More: Second Edition
3D Origami Diamonds
3D Origami Antidiamonds
3D Origami Pyramids
A Plethora of Polyhedra in Origami: Third Edition
Classic Polyhedra Origami
A Constellation of Origami Polyhedra
Origami Polyhedra Design

General Origami

Origami Fold-by-Fold
DC Super Heroes Origami
Origami Worldwide
Teach Yourself Origami: Third Edition
Christmas Origami: Second Edition
Storytime Origami
Origami Inside-Out: Third Edition

Dollar Bill Origami

Dollar Origami Treasures: Second Edition
Dollar Bill Animals in Origami: Second Revised Edition
Dollar Bill Origami
Easy Dollar Bill Origami

Simple Origami

Fun and Simple Origami: 101 Easy-to-Fold Projects: Second Edition
Origami Twelve Days of Christmas: And Santa, Too!
Super Simple Origami
Easy Dollar Bill Origami
Easy Origami
Easy Origami 2
Easy Origami 3
Easy Origami Coloring Book
Easy Origami Animals
Easy Origami Polar Animals
Easy Origami Ocean Animals
Easy Origami Woodland Animals
Easy Origami Jungle Animals
Meditative Origami

Origami Symphony No. 11

Folding on Land, Air and Sea

Antroll Publishing Company

John Montroll

To Tim and Jennifer

Origami Symphony No. 11: *Folding on Land, Air and Sea*

ISBN-10: 1-877656-67-4
ISBN-13: 978-1-877656-67-5

Antroll Publishing Company

Introduction

Welcome to the world premier of the Eleventh Origami Symphony! Modeled after musical symphonies in four movements, this brings origami to another level. South American mammals, colorful jungle birds, a series of pyramids and celestial shapes, along with fun sea creatures adds to the variety and enjoyment of origami.

A Chinchilla, Anteater and Llama from South America come to life. Jungle birds include a Vulture, Flamingo and Hoopoe. A Jackstone and Heptahedron show a complex side to geometric origami. Cute sea creatures include a Triggerfish, Leatherback Turtle and Hermit Crab. The 36 models in this origami symphony use innovative techniques to capture the subjects in a detailed life-like manner.

Great care in design was used so the models are as easy to fold as possible, given their complexity. Most of the models are folded in under 30 steps. Only a few require more, such as some of the polyhedra in the trio and the last few sea creatures. The Hermit Crab, last model in this collection, is diagrammed in 50 steps, the most of any model shown here. All the models are easily foldable from standard origami paper. The efficiency and ease in folding adds a life-force to these works, representing simplicity within complexity. It also allows for plenty of freedom of interpretation for any folder to enjoy.

The diagrams are drawn in the internationally approved Randlett-Yoshizawa style. You can use any kind of square paper for these models, but the best results will be achieved with standard origami paper, which is colored on one side and white on the other (in the diagrams in this book, the shading represents the colored side). Large sheets, such as nine inches squared, are easier to use than small ones.

Origami supplies can be found in arts and craft shops, or at Dover Publications online: www.doverpublications.com. You can also visit OrigamiUSA at www.origamiusa.org for origami supplies and other related information including an extensive list of local, national, and international origami groups.

Please follow me on Instagram @montrollorigami to see posts of my origami.

I give special thanks to Jon Herrity for the photographs of the models. I also thank the folders who continued to encourage me to develop the presentation of origami through an origami symphony.

I hope you enjoy Origami Symphony No. 11.

John Montroll
www.johnmontroll.com

Contents

★ Simple
★★ Intermediate
★★★ Complex
★★★★ Very Complex

First Movement
Allegro: Footsteps of South American Mammals

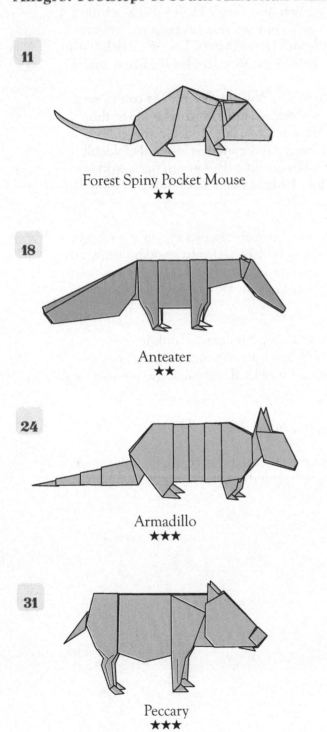

11

Forest Spiny Pocket Mouse
★★

18

Anteater
★★

24

Armadillo
★★★

31

Peccary
★★★

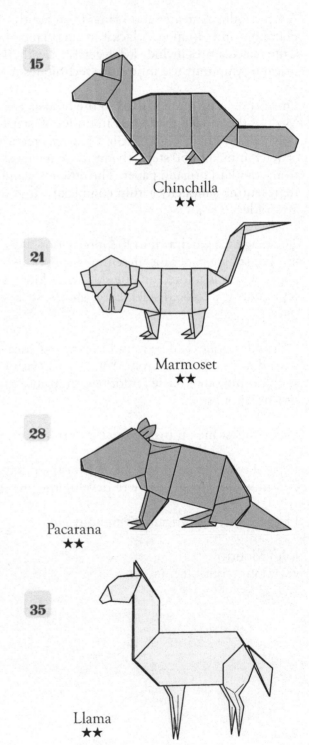

15

Chinchilla
★★

21

Marmoset
★★

28

Pacarana
★★

35

Llama
★★

Second Movement
Andante: Parade of Jungle Birds

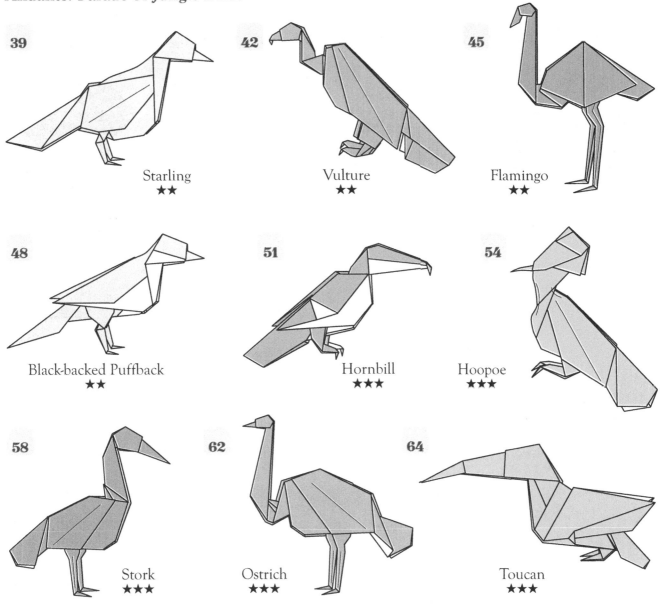

39 Starling
★★

42 Vulture
★★

45 Flamingo
★★

48 Black-backed Puffback
★★

51 Hornbill
★★★

54 Hoopoe
★★★

58 Stork
★★★

62 Ostrich
★★★

64 Toucan
★★★

Third Movement
Minuet of Triangular Pyramids with a Trio of Spherical Gems

68 Mound
★

70 Tetrahedron
★

72 Crown
★★

75 Pinnacle
★★

78 Peak
★

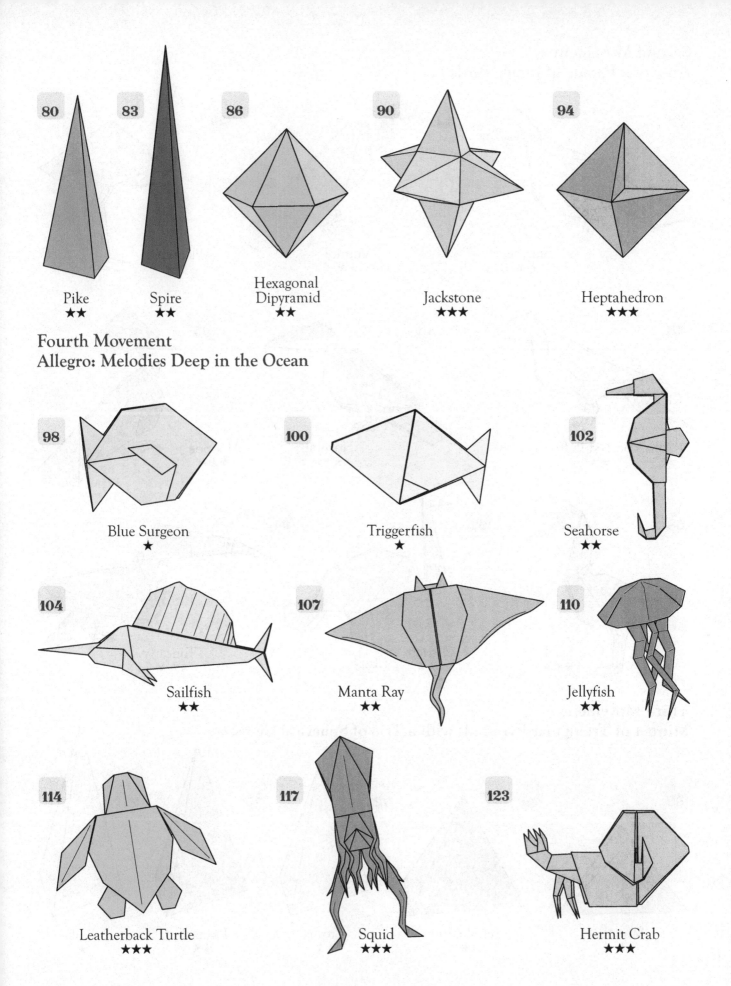

80 Pike
★★

83 Spire
★★

86 Hexagonal Dipyramid
★★

90 Jackstone
★★★

94 Heptahedron
★★★

Fourth Movement
Allegro: Melodies Deep in the Ocean

98 Blue Surgeon
★

100 Triggerfish
★

102 Seahorse
★★

104 Sailfish
★★

107 Manta Ray
★★

110 Jellyfish
★★

114 Leatherback Turtle
★★★

117 Squid
★★★

123 Hermit Crab
★★★

Symbols

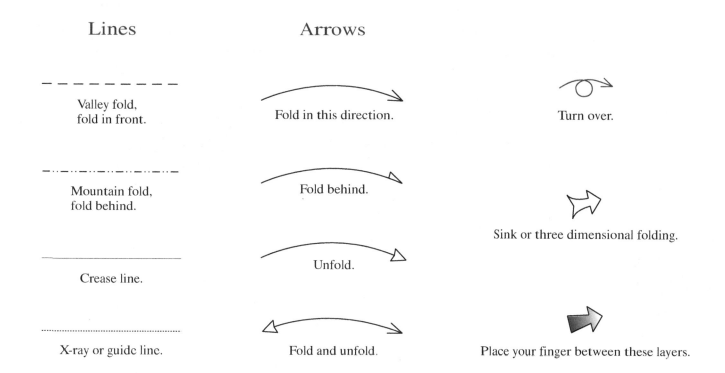

Lines	Arrows	
Valley fold, fold in front.	Fold in this direction.	Turn over.
Mountain fold, fold behind.	Fold behind.	Sink or three dimensional folding.
Crease line.	Unfold.	
X-ray or guide line.	Fold and unfold.	Place your finger between these layers.

Geometry with Origami Design

Origami design has always been a favorite topic for me. Use of geometry allows for different spaces that can enhance design. Given a square sheet of paper, the corners are at 90°. Half of that is 45° and half again is 22.5°. Most origami animals, throughout the history of origami design, are structured around the 22.5° angle.

For a long time, I have used 30° and hence also 60° and 15° in my work. When a corner of the square is trisected, it yields 30°. Models based on 30° (and 60° or 15°) present a different space for origami design. Some of the models from this origami symphony which use these angles include the Vulture, Triggerfish, Sailfish, and Jellyfish. The Triggerfish is basically two equilateral triangles for the body, creating a diamond shape with a few appendages for the fins and tail.

For this work, I have explored angles that occur when the corner of the square is divided into fifths. This yields 18° and 36°. These angles can lead to a new set of origami models. The Hornbill and Leatherback Turtle are based on 18°. For the turtle, these angles create a pleasant shape where the legs and body proportions fit together well, with efficiency in folding. The Flamingo uses 18° in a spectacular way. While the traditional bird base is based on 22.5° angles, I have created a modified bird base based on 18°. This forms longer and thinner legs for the Flamingo, giving it more character, still with ease in folding.

I have even combined 15° and 18° as different parts for the Stork and Ostrich. This illustrates the richness of origami design.

Some of the polyhedra from the third movement also use angles of 15°, 30°, 60° along with 36°. Between the polyhedra and animals, the use of these angles add elegance to origami design.

Origami Symphony No. 11

Let's travel on land, air and sea as we explore more possibilities through origami. Mammals from South America, tropical birds, pyramids on land along with celestial bodies in the sky, and zany ocean creatures entertain and challenge us.

Starting in the Footsteps of South America, the first movement opens with a Forest Spiny Pocket Mouse scampering between the rocks. Fold the creature quickly before it runs away. A Chinchilla is jumping around while an Anteater is sleeping and waiting for its next meal. A few Marmosets are spotted playing in the treetops. An Armadillo is showing off its swimming skills as a Pacarana slowly walks by. After some Peccarys are playing in mud holes, a Llama greets us as the movement ends.

The second movement, Andante: Parade of Jungle Birds, fills the ground, trees and skies with beautiful birds. Starlings and Vultures are flying around. A modified bird base is formed into a Flamingo with very long, thin legs. A Black-backed Puffback and Hornbill demonstrate the use of both sides of the paper for effective color-change patterns. A Hoopoe, Stork, and Ostrich are folded from different

structures but have similar wings. Noisy Toucans fill the treetops.

The third movement begins with a minuet of Triangular Pyramids. The bases for each pyramid is an equilateral triangle and each pyramid grows taller and taller. As the pyramids are on land, the trio of Spherical Gems fills the skies. This includes the Jackstone and Heptahedron.

The fourth movement, Allegro: Melodies Deep in the Ocean show a variety of sea creatures. The easy-to-fold Blue Surgeon and Triggerfish are swimming in the coral reefs. A Seahorse is enjoying the ocean vegetation. Deeper in the ocean, watch carefully as Sailfish swim by quickly. Manta Rays, Jellyfish and Leatherback Turtles fill the seas with color and majesty. Complex origami models finish this origami symphony with a Squid glowing in the dark and a Hermit Crab chirping.

By Folding on Land, Air and Sea, many subjects are covered. The South American mammals, jungle birds, pyramids and spherical gems, along with sea creatures show the richness and possibilities of origami. I hope you enjoy this work.

First Movement

Allegro: Footsteps of South American Mammals

In origami, mammals represent the complex, earthy and muscular side of design. Watch carefully as a Forest Spiny Pocket Mouse runs through the rainforest. A Chinchilla jumps around a sleepy Anteater. High in the treetops, a small Marmoset is dropping fruit for an Armadillo. A large Pacarana is hiding between rocks in the rainforest, hoping to avoid a nearby Peccary. Llamas greet you as the movement ends, and guide you through rocky terrain to the second movement.

Forest Spiny Pocket Mouse

The forest spiny pocket mouse is a small mouse with a long tail and body length around 7 to 8 inches long. It is named for the spines on its back. This mouse lives in rainforests and rocky desert landscapes. Hidden during the day, families sleep in burrows and at night feed on grasses and shrubs.

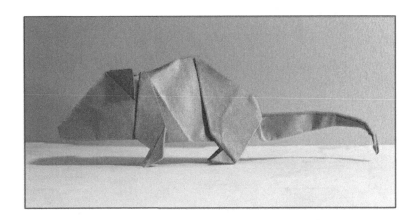

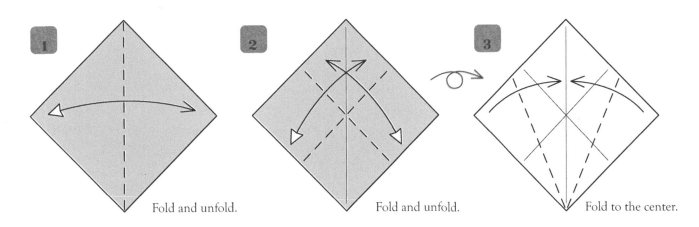

1. Fold and unfold.

2. Fold and unfold.

3. Fold to the center.

4

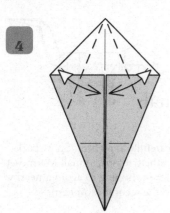

Fold to the center and unfold.

5

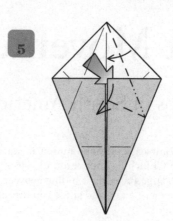

Mountain-fold along the crease for this squash fold.

6

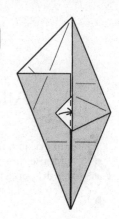

Tuck inside.

7

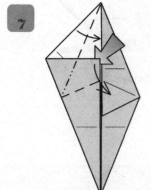

Repeat steps 5–6 on the left.

8

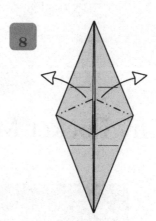

Unfold.

9

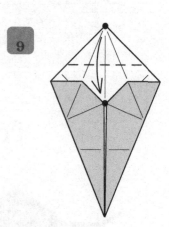

10

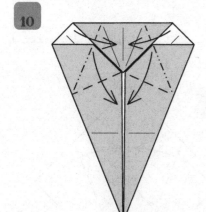

Make squash folds.

11

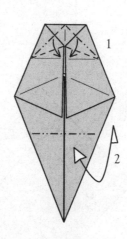

1
2

1. Make squash folds.
2. Fold and unfold along the crease.

12

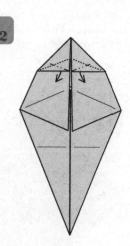

Make reverse folds.

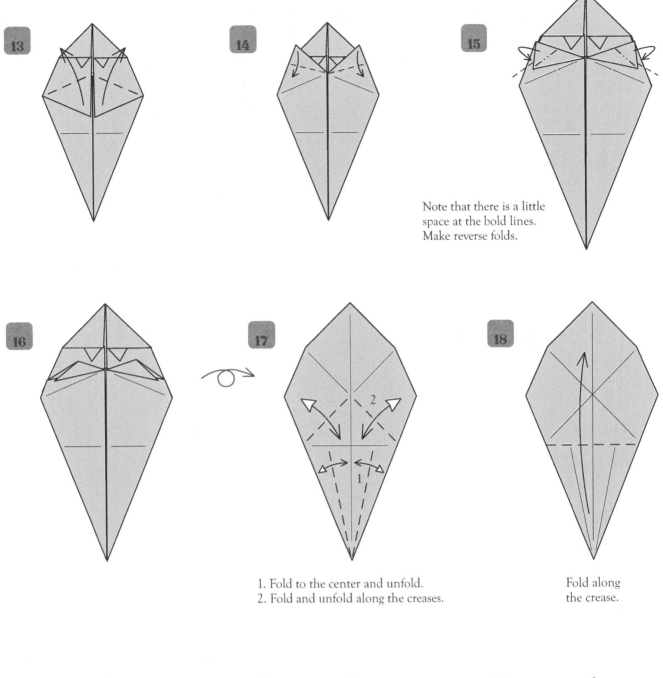

Note that there is a little
space at the bold lines.
Make reverse folds.

1. Fold to the center and unfold.
2. Fold and unfold along the creases.

Fold along
the crease.

Fold and unfold.

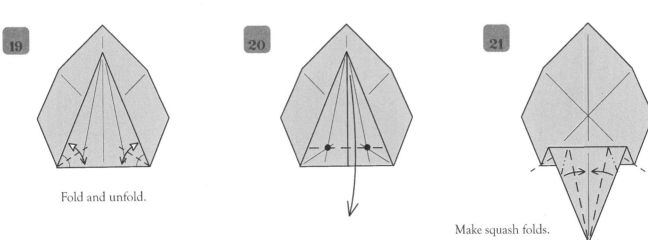

Make squash folds.

22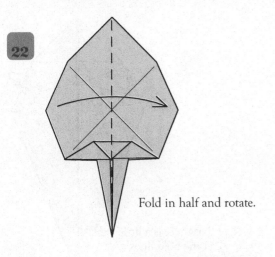

Fold in half and rotate.

23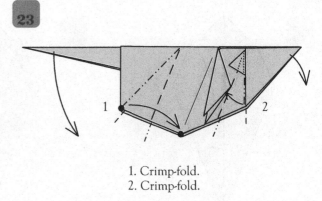

1. Crimp-fold.
2. Crimp-fold.

24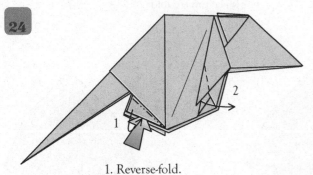

1. Reverse-fold.
2. Outside-reverse-fold.
Repeat behind.

25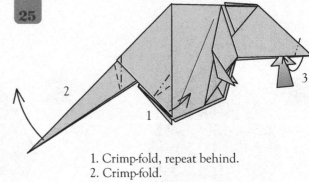

1. Crimp-fold, repeat behind.
2. Crimp-fold.
3. Reverse-fold.

26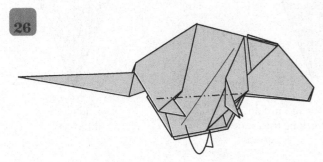

Fold inside and repeat behind.

27

1. Shape the back.
2. Curl the tail.
3. Fold the ears, repeat behind.

28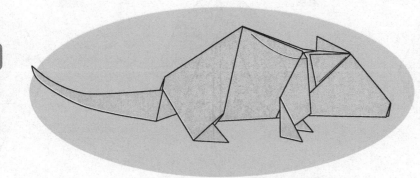

Forest Spiny Pocket Mouse

Chinchilla

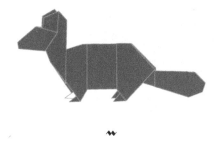

Native to the Andes Mountains of Northern Chile, chinchillas are related to guinea pigs and porcupines. Their thick fur protects them from the extreme cold in the mountains. Found in large colonies, these social rodents burrow in underground tunnels. Feeding on grasses and insects, the chinchilla holds its food in its front paws to nibble. They can jump six feet and live up to twenty years.

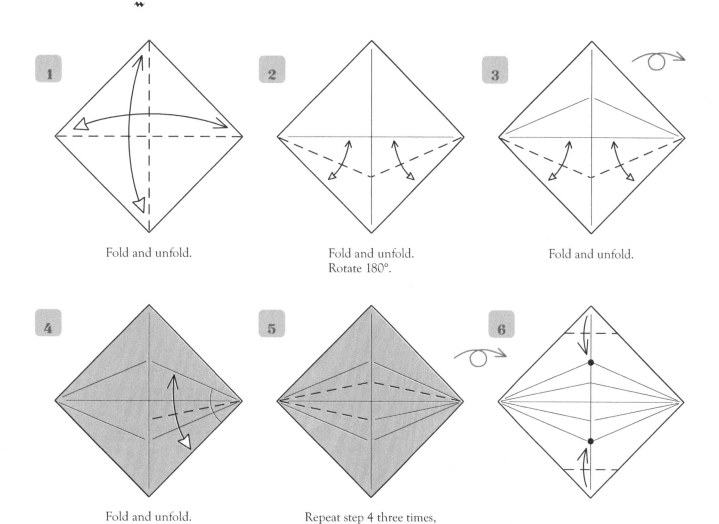

1 Fold and unfold.

2 Fold and unfold. Rotate 180°.

3 Fold and unfold.

4 Fold and unfold.

5 Repeat step 4 three times, on the left and above.

6

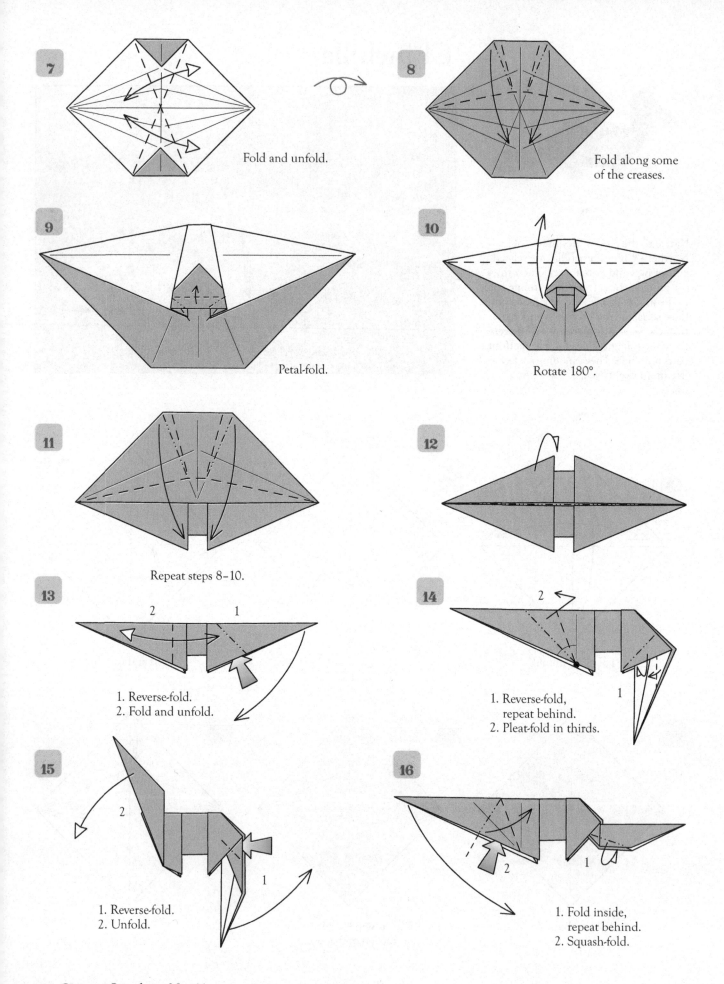

7 Fold and unfold.

8 Fold along some of the creases.

9 Petal-fold.

10 Rotate 180°.

11 Repeat steps 8–10.

12

13
2   1
1. Reverse-fold.
2. Fold and unfold.

14
2
1. Reverse-fold, repeat behind.
2. Pleat-fold in thirds.
1

15
2
1. Reverse-fold.
2. Unfold.
1

16
2   1
1. Fold inside, repeat behind.
2. Squash-fold.

17

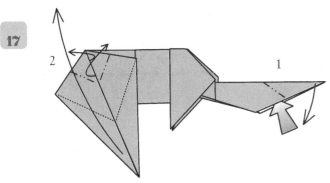

1. Reverse-fold.
2. Wrap around and petal-fold.

18

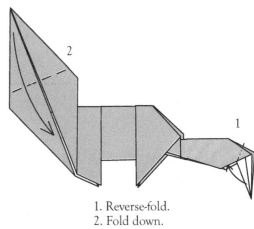

1. Reverse-fold.
2. Fold down.

19

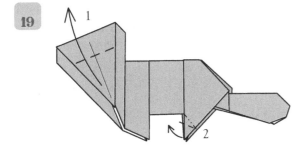

1. Fold up.
2. Crimp-fold, repeat behind.

20

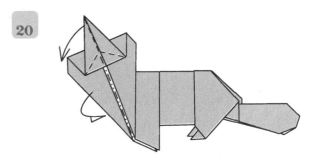

Rabbit-ear and fold behind.

21

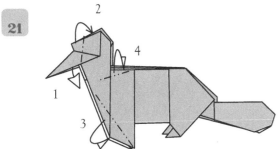

1. Pull out from inside, repeat behind.
2. Reverse-fold.
3. Tuck inside, repeat behind.
4. Fold inside with a small hidden
   squash fold, repeat behind.

22

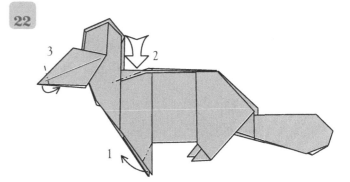

1. Reverse-fold, repeat behind.
2. Sink.
3. Reverse-fold.

23

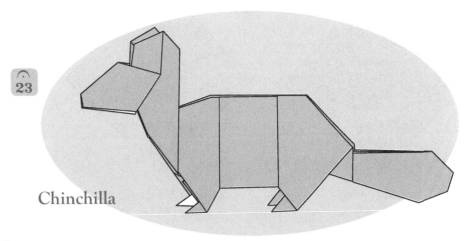

Chinchilla

Anteater

Anteaters dine on 30,000 insects every day. They like ants, termites and other insects. Anteaters also eat fruit and bird eggs. They have no teeth and use their clawed front toes to break apart insect nests. Their long tongue is covered with spines. Found in grasslands, savannas, and tropical forests, they spend 15 hours a day sleeping. They usually move slowly but can swim and climb trees.

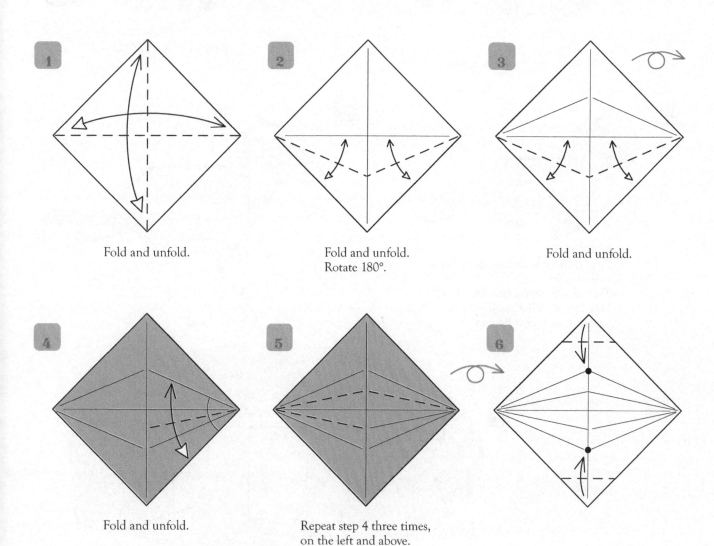

1. Fold and unfold.

2. Fold and unfold. Rotate 180°.

3. Fold and unfold.

4. Fold and unfold.

5. Repeat step 4 three times, on the left and above.

6.

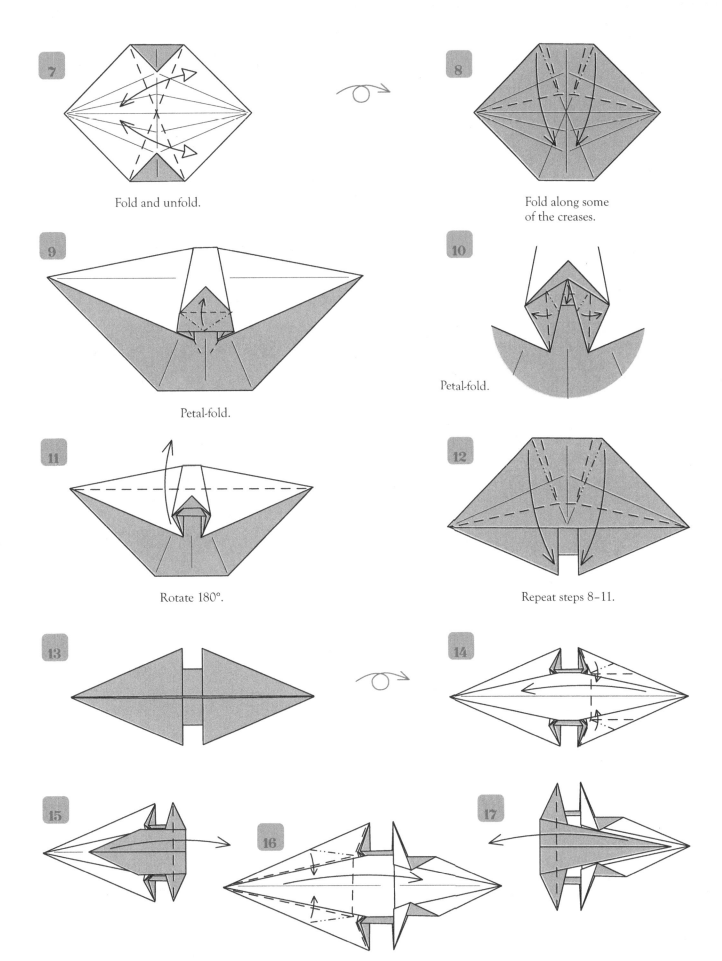

7 Fold and unfold.

8 Fold along some of the creases.

9 Petal-fold.

10 Petal-fold.

11 Rotate 180°.

12 Repeat steps 8–11.

13

14

15

16

17

18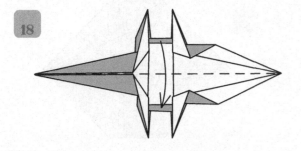

19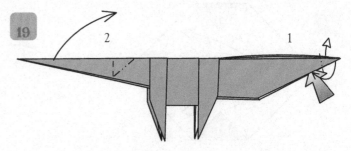

1. Spread and make a reverse fold.
2. Crimp-fold.

20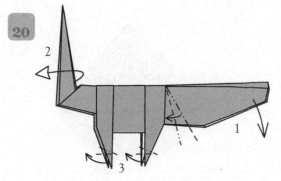

1. Crimp-fold.
2. Pull out, repeat behind.
3. Make crimp folds, repeat behind.

21

1. Reverse-fold, repeat behind.
2. Shape the legs, repeat behind.
3. Reverse-fold.

22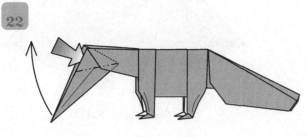

Reverse-fold.

23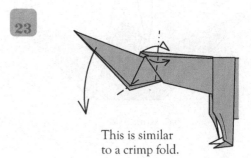

This is similar
to a crimp fold.

24

1. Reverse-fold, repeat behind.
2. Fold inside, repeat behind.
3. Reverse-fold.

25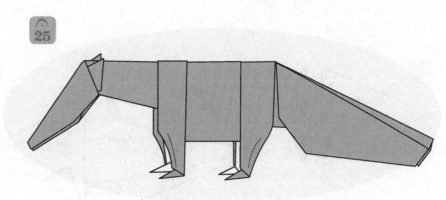

Anteater

Marmoset

The marmoset is the smallest monkey. Found in tropical forests or rainforests, they live in treetops. Their long tail is used for balance as they scamper from branch to branch, but cannot grasp with it. They live in social groups called troops, with an average size of 6 to 15 moneys. With sharp teeth, they saw holes in trees to feed on tree sap. They also dine on fruits, insects, frogs and other small animals. They communicate with many vocal sounds.

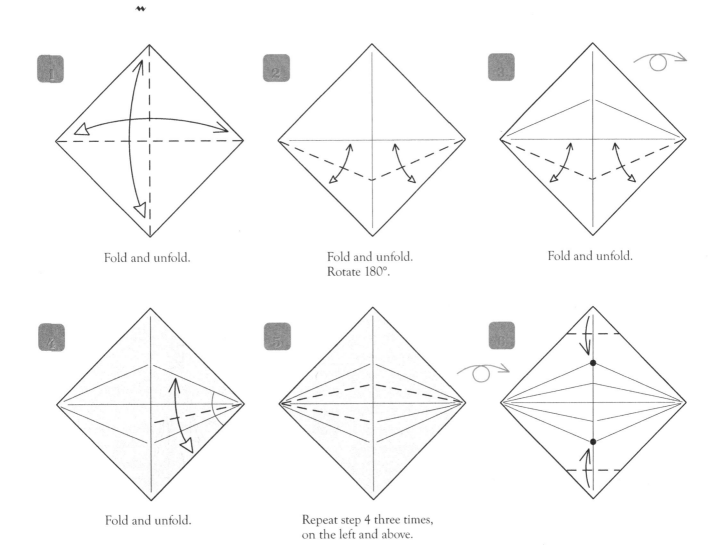

1

Fold and unfold.

2

Fold and unfold.
Rotate 180°.

3

Fold and unfold.

4

Fold and unfold.

5

Repeat step 4 three times,
on the left and above.

6

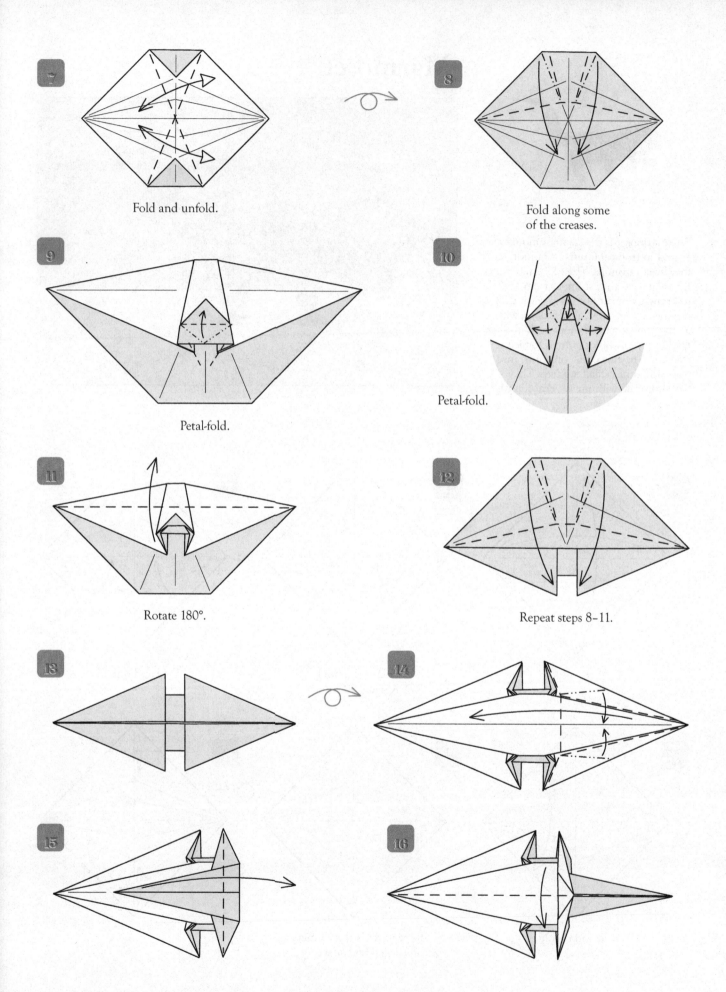

7 Fold and unfold.

8 Fold along some of the creases.

9 Petal-fold.

10 Petal-fold.

11 Rotate 180°.

12 Repeat steps 8–11.

13

14

15

16

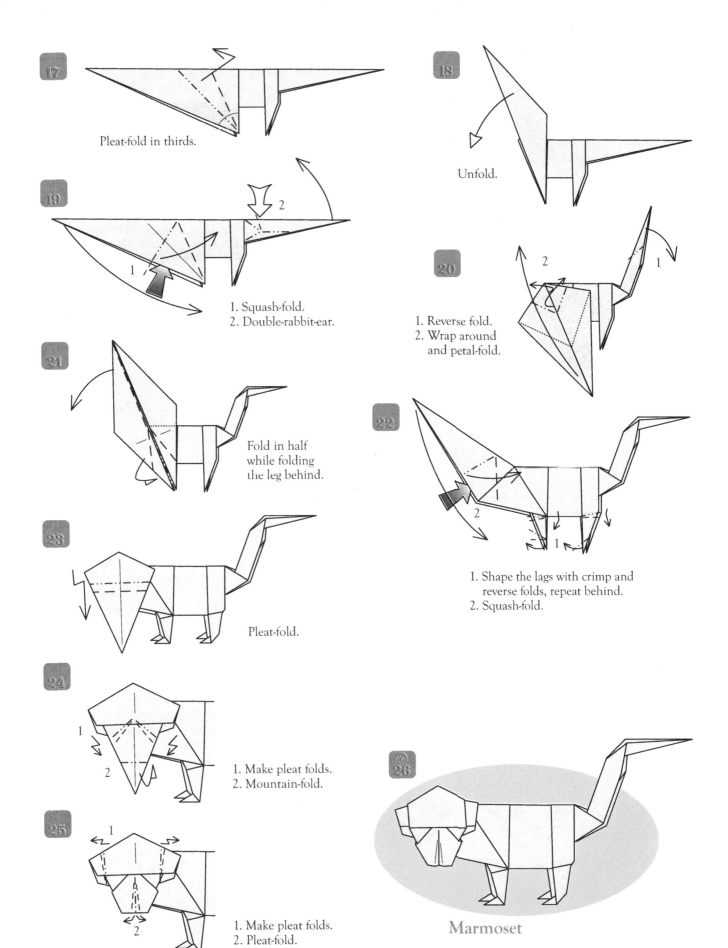

17 Pleat-fold in thirds.

18 Unfold.

19
1. Squash-fold.
2. Double-rabbit-ear.

20
1. Reverse fold.
2. Wrap around and petal-fold.

21 Fold in half while folding the leg behind.

22
1. Shape the legs with crimp and reverse folds, repeat behind.
2. Squash-fold.

23 Pleat-fold.

24
1. Make pleat folds.
2. Mountain-fold.

25
1. Make pleat folds.
2. Pleat-fold.

26 Marmoset

Armadillo

Armadillo is from Spanish for "little armored one". Armadillos like to dig for food which includes insects, small animals, and fruit. They will share their burrows with rats, snakes and turtles, but not other armadillos. They dig burrows so they can hide and sleep during the day. They will share their burrows with rats, snakes, and turtles, but not other armadillos. Armadillos like to swim.

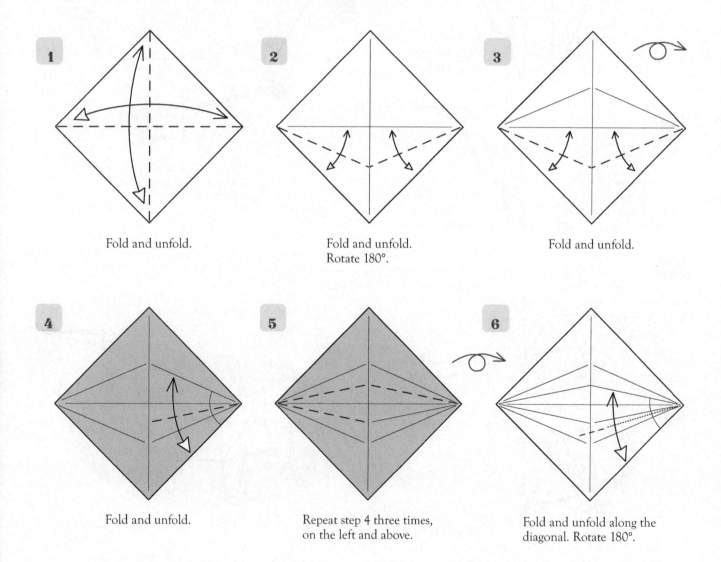

1 Fold and unfold.

2 Fold and unfold. Rotate 180°.

3 Fold and unfold.

4 Fold and unfold.

5 Repeat step 4 three times, on the left and above.

6 Fold and unfold along the diagonal. Rotate 180°.

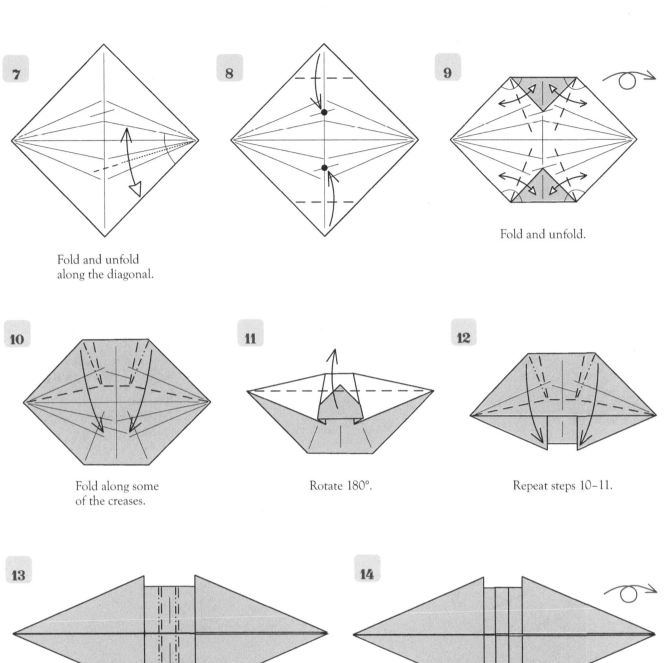

7

Fold and unfold
along the diagonal.

8

9

Fold and unfold.

10

Fold along some
of the creases.

11

Rotate 180°.

12

Repeat steps 10–11.

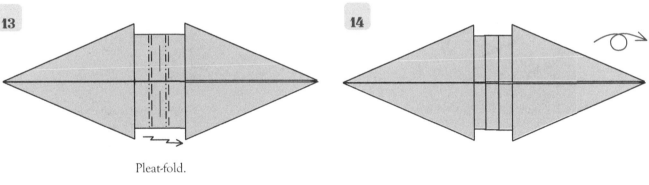

13

Pleat-fold.

14

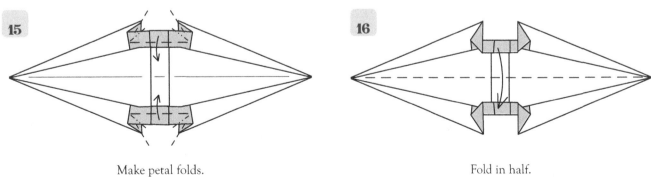

15

Make petal folds.

16

Fold in half.

17

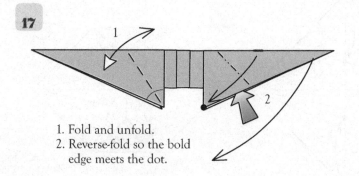

1. Fold and unfold.
2. Reverse-fold so the bold edge meets the dot.

18

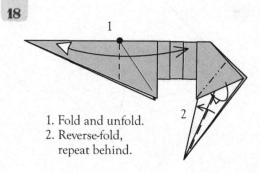

1. Fold and unfold.
2. Reverse-fold, repeat behind.

19

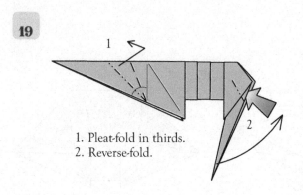

1. Pleat-fold in thirds.
2. Reverse-fold.

20

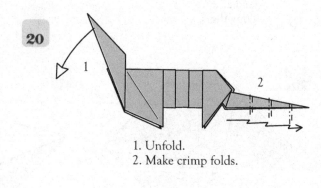

1. Unfold.
2. Make crimp folds.

21

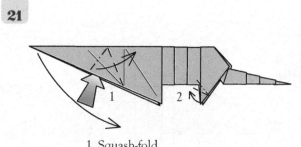

1. Squash-fold.
2. Crimp-fold, repeat behind.

22

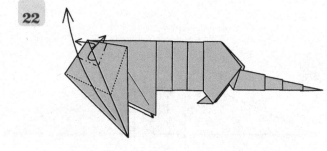

Wrap around and petal-fold.

23

24

25

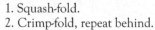

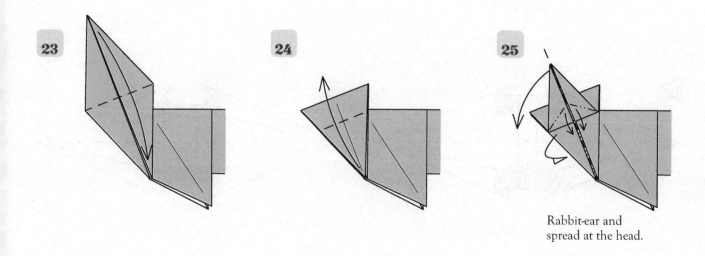

Rabbit-ear and spread at the head.

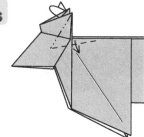

This is similar to a reverse fold. Repeat behind.

 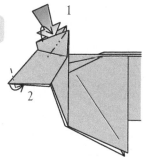

1. Reverse-fold.
2. Reverse-fold.

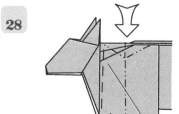

Push in at the top and make a crimp fold.

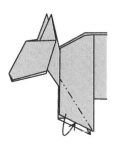

Reverse-fold, repeat behind.

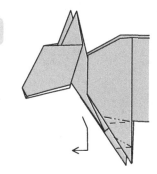

Make crimp folds, repeat behind.

 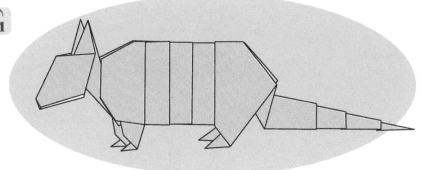

Armadillo

Pacarana

The pacarana is a chunky rodent with a large head. Found in rainforests, they sleep during the day between rocks or in caves by trees. They are active at night and feed on fruits, plants, and vegetables. While eating, they sit and grasp food with their front paws. They move slowly and the young climb trees. In zoos, they are surprisingly friendly to humans and especially enjoy corn on the cob.

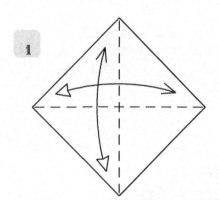

1

Fold and unfold.

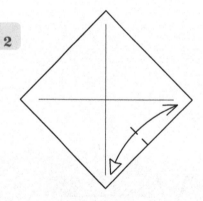

2

Fold and unfold on the bottom right.

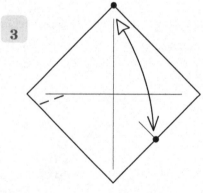

3

Fold and unfold on the left so the dots meet.

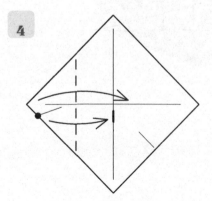

4

Fold so the dot meets the crease.

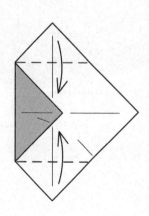

5

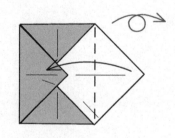

6

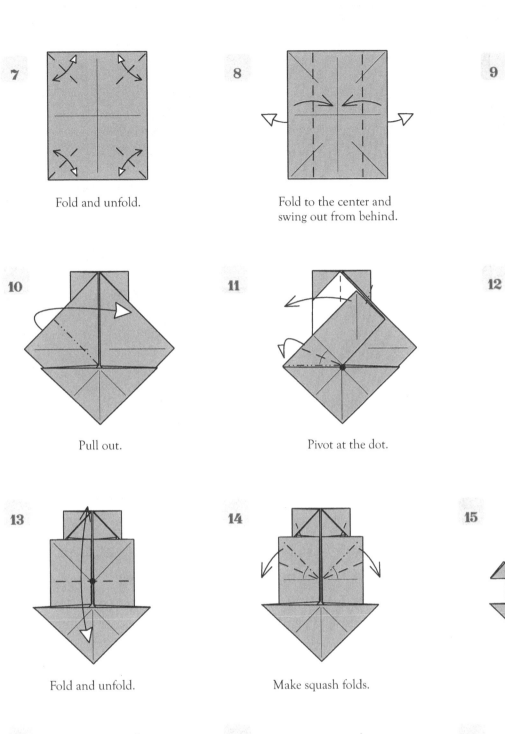

7 Fold and unfold.

8 Fold to the center and swing out from behind.

9 Petal-fold and swing out from behind.

10 Pull out.

11 Pivot at the dot.

12 Repeat steps 10–11 on the right.

13 Fold and unfold.

14 Make squash folds.

15 Rotate 90°.

16 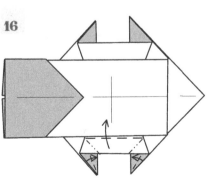 Petal-fold.

17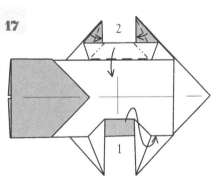
1. Tuck inside.
2. Repeat steps 16–17 on the top.

18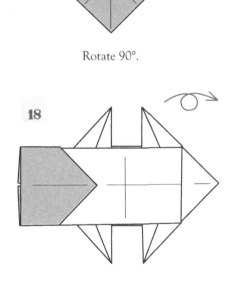

19

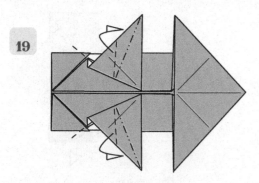

Thin the legs.

20

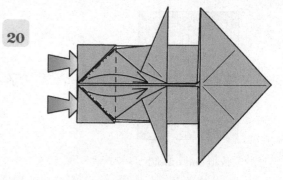

Make squash folds.

21

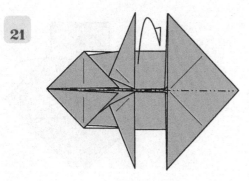

Fold in half.

22

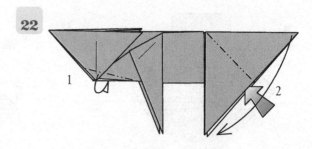

1. Fold inside, repeat behind.
2. Reverse-fold.

23

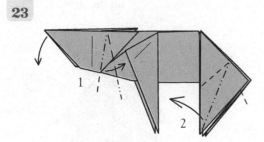

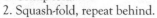

1. Crimp-fold.
2. Squash-fold, repeat behind.

24

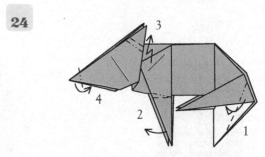

1. Reverse-fold.
2. Crimp-fold.
3. Crimp-fold.
4. Reverse-fold.
Repeat behind at 1, 2, and 3.

25

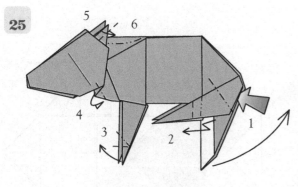

1. Reverse-fold.
2. Crimp-fold.
3. Crimp-fold.
4. Fold inside.
5. Open the ears.
6. Shape the back.
Repeat behind at 2, 3, 4, and 5.

26

Pacarana

Peccary

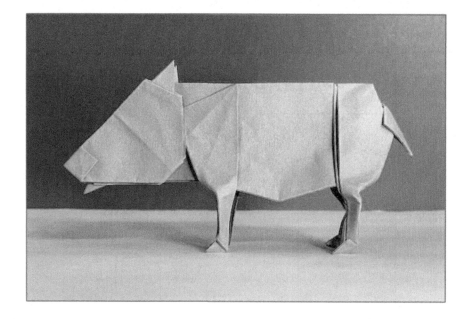

Found in desert scrub, woodlands and rainforests, the peccary is very intelligent and lives in herds of up to 50 members. Their sense of smell is very good and they can smell food buried in soil. They eat cactus, berries, seeds, insects and other small animals. They look like pigs but they are not. Their coat is coarse and bristled. They dig up large mud holes, or wallows, which frogs enjoy, too.

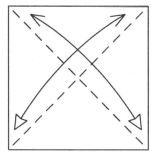

Fold and unfold.

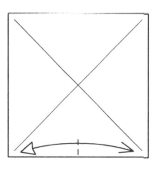

Fold and unfold on the bottom.

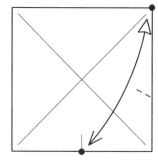

Fold and unfold on the right.

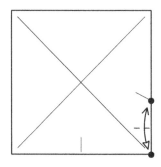

Fold and unfold on the right.

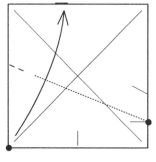

Bring the dot to the top edge and crease on the left.

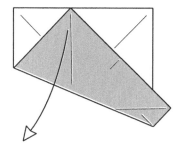

Unfold.

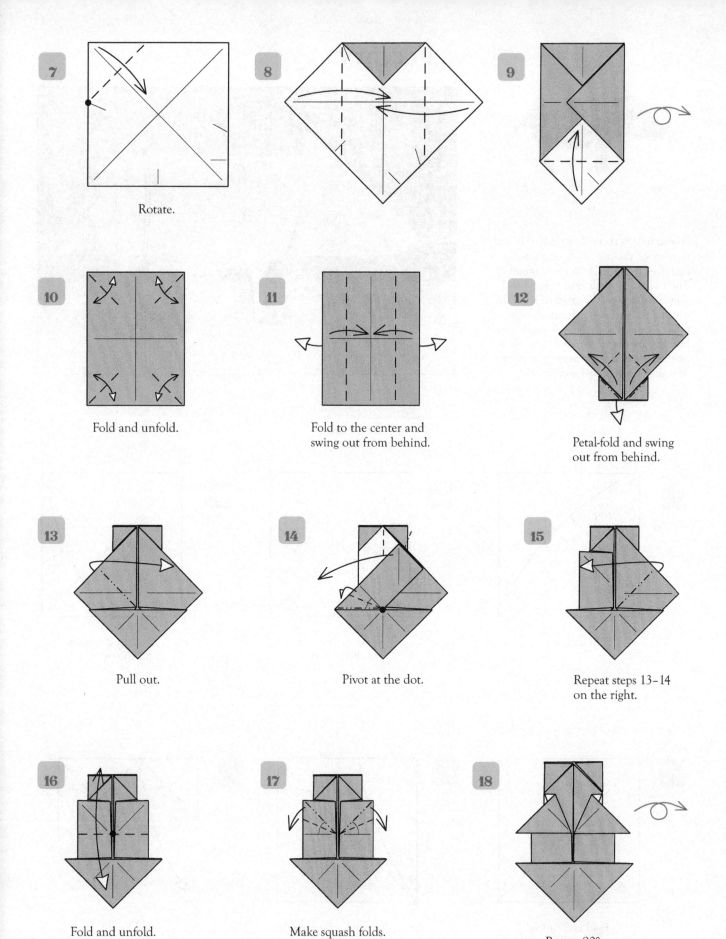

7 Rotate.

8

9

10 Fold and unfold.

11 Fold to the center and swing out from behind.

12 Petal-fold and swing out from behind.

13 Pull out.

14 Pivot at the dot.

15 Repeat steps 13–14 on the right.

16 Fold and unfold.

17 Make squash folds.

18 Rotate 90°.

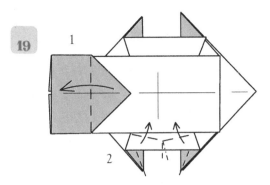

19

1. Fold the top layer.
2. This is a combination of squash folds.

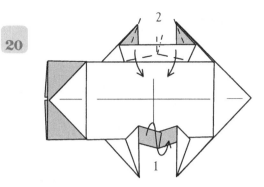

20

1. Tuck inside.
2. Repeat steps 19–20 on the top.

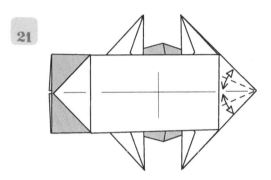

21

Fold and unfold.

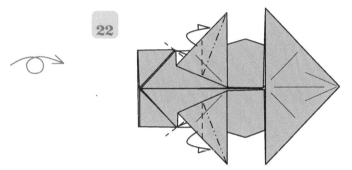

22

Thin the legs.

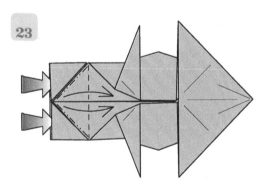

23

Make squash folds.

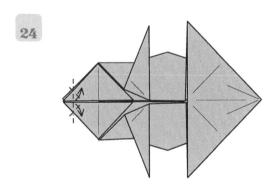

24

This is similar to a petal fold.

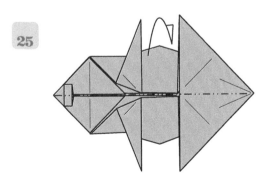

25

Fold in half.

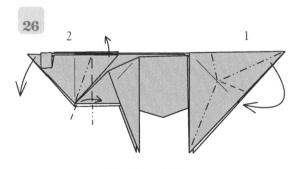

26

1. Double-rabbit-ear.
2. Crimp-fold.

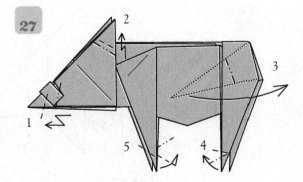

27

1. Crimp-fold.
2. Crimp-fold.
3. Reverse-fold.
4. Squash-fold.
5. Squash-fold.
Repeat behind at 2, 4, and 5.

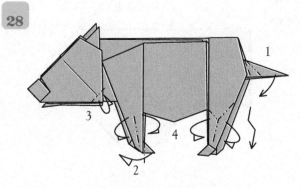

28

1. Crimp-fold.
2. Mountain-fold.
3. Fold inside.
4. Shape the legs.
Repeat behind at 2, 3, and 4.

29

Peccary

Llama

Llamas are social and intelligent creatures. They live in herds of 20 to 100. Llamas have been domesticated and are easy to train. Llamas are used as pack animals as they are friendly to flocks of sheep and goats and will chase off predators. They can carry heavy goods over long distances. They walk gently on the ground and are adept on rocky terrain.

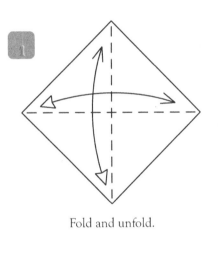

Fold and unfold.

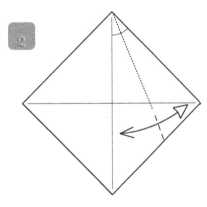

Fold and unfold on the edge.

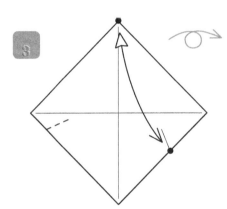

Fold and unfold on the edge.

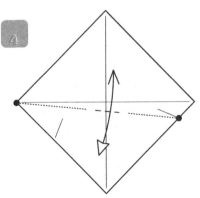

Fold and unfold on the diagonal.

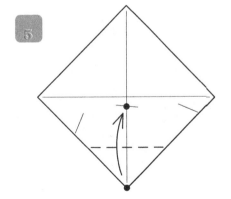

The dots will meet.

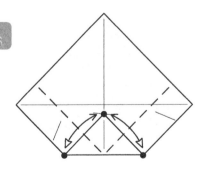

Fold and unfold.

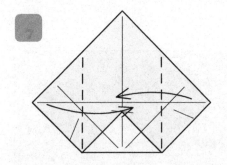

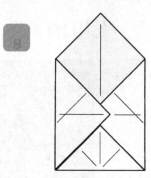

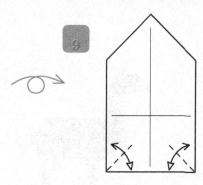

Fold and unfold.

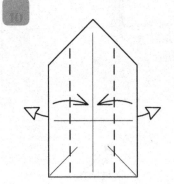

Fold to the center and
swing out from behind.

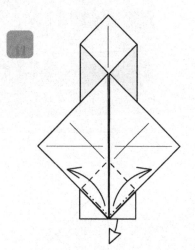

Petal-fold and swing
out from behind.

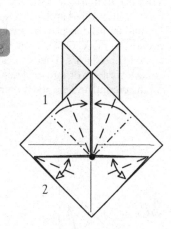

1. Pivot at the dot.
2. Fold and unfold
   the top flap.

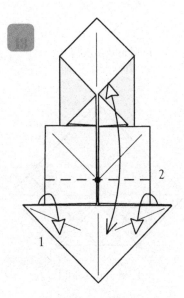

1. Wrap around.
2. Fold and unfold.

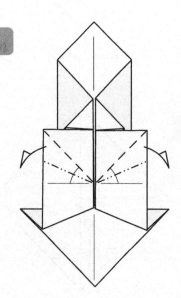

Make squash folds.

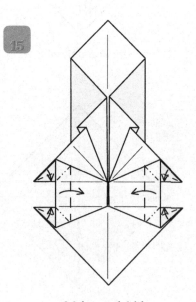

Make petal folds.

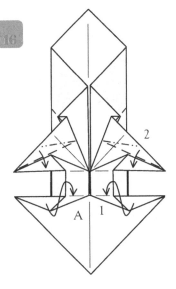

1. Tuck under region A.
2. Make squash folds.

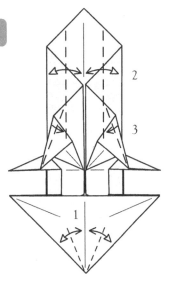

1. Fold and unfold.
2. Fold and unfold.
3. Fold on the left and right.

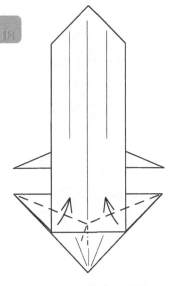

Make a small pleat fold.

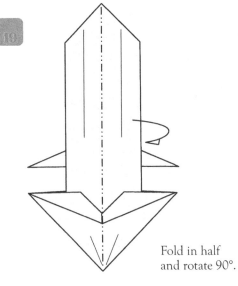

Fold in half
and rotate 90°.

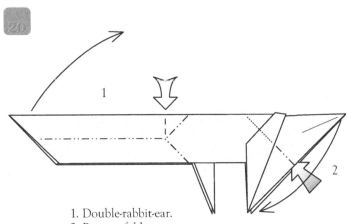

1. Double-rabbit-ear.
2. Reverse-fold.

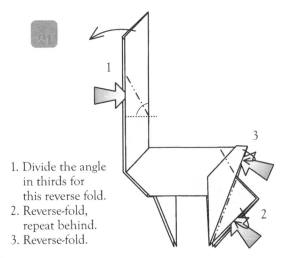

1. Divide the angle
   in thirds for
   this reverse fold.
2. Reverse-fold,
   repeat behind.
3. Reverse-fold.

1. Crimp-fold the head.
2. Crimp-fold the tail.

Llama **37**

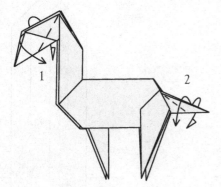

23

1. Outside-reverse-fold.
2. Outside-reverse-fold.

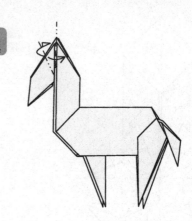

24

Crimp-fold.

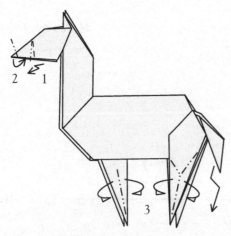

25

1. Crimp-fold.
2. Reverse-fold.
3. Shape the legs, repeat behind.

26

Llama

Second Movement

Andante: Parade of Jungle Birds

Tropical birds take us to the skies. In origami, birds represent elegance and beauty. Starlings entertain us with their loud and noisy songs. Vultures soar above while large flocks of Flamingos wade in the swamps. A Hornbill, Hoopoe, and Black-backed Puffback fly around in search of insects. Storks march through shallow water and Ostriches are keeping watch in the savannas. With large bills but small wings, colorful Toucans are gathering fruit.

Starling

Starlings are noisy and social birds. They can mimic other bird calls. At around 8 inches long, they walk on the ground rather than hop. Starlings feed on insects, seeds, grains and fruit. They dig for bugs in the ground with their beak. Flying in large flocks, they migrate for hundreds of miles.

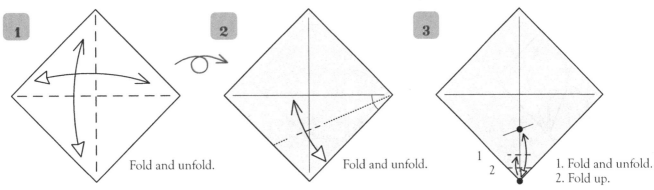

1 Fold and unfold.

2 Fold and unfold.

3 1. Fold and unfold.
2. Fold up.

Starling **39**

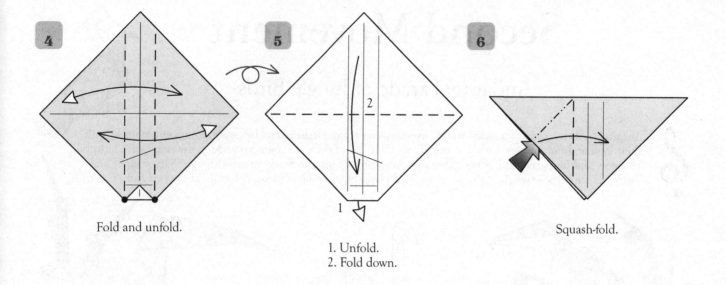

4 Fold and unfold.

5
1. Unfold.
2. Fold down.

6 Squash-fold.

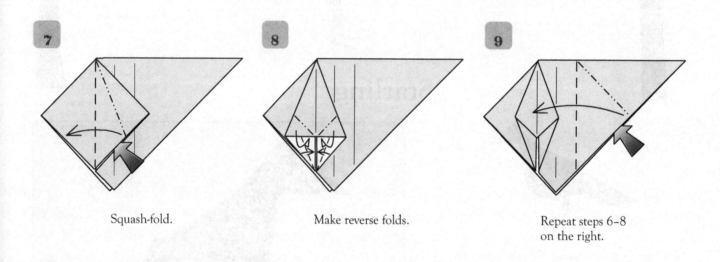

7 Squash-fold.

8 Make reverse folds.

9 Repeat steps 6–8 on the right.

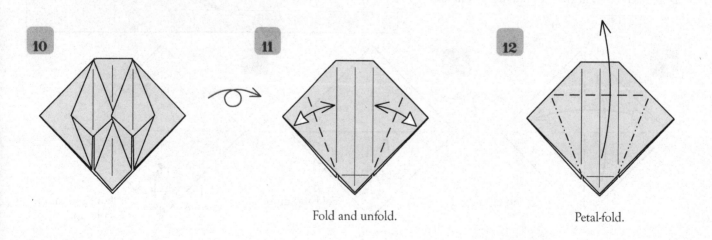

10

11 Fold and unfold.

12 Petal-fold.

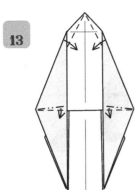

13

Slide the paper.

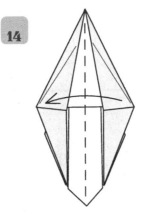

14

Fold in half and rotate.

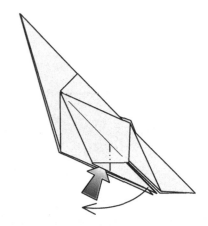

15

Reverse-fold and repeat behind.

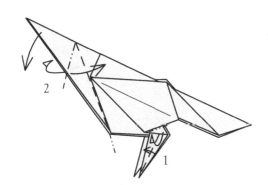

16

1. Thin the leg and repeat on the other side, repeat behind.
2. Crimp-fold.

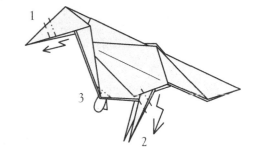

17

1. Crimp-fold.
2. Crimp-fold, repeat behind.
3. Fold inside, repeat behind.

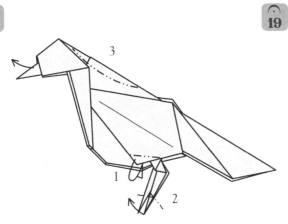

18

1. Slide inside, repeat behind.
2. Crimp-fold, repeat behind.
3. Shape the back.

19

Starling

Starling **41**

Vulture

Vultures are well adapted for feeding on carrion. Their hooked beak makes it easy to tear through the food. There are no feathers on the head, to protect them when eating. Vultures like to fly through thermals, where hot air is rising, so they don't need to flap their wings. Finding food is easy for them, as they follow other animals that know where to find food.

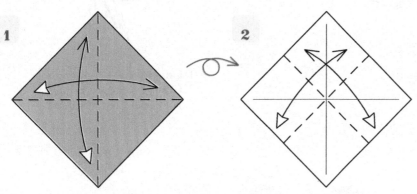

1

Fold and unfold.

2

Fold and unfold.

3

Fold and unfold.

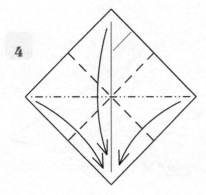

4

Fold along the creases.

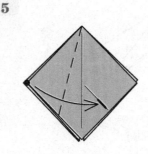

5

Fold the top layer. Bring the dot to the line.

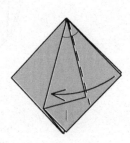

6

Fold the top layer.

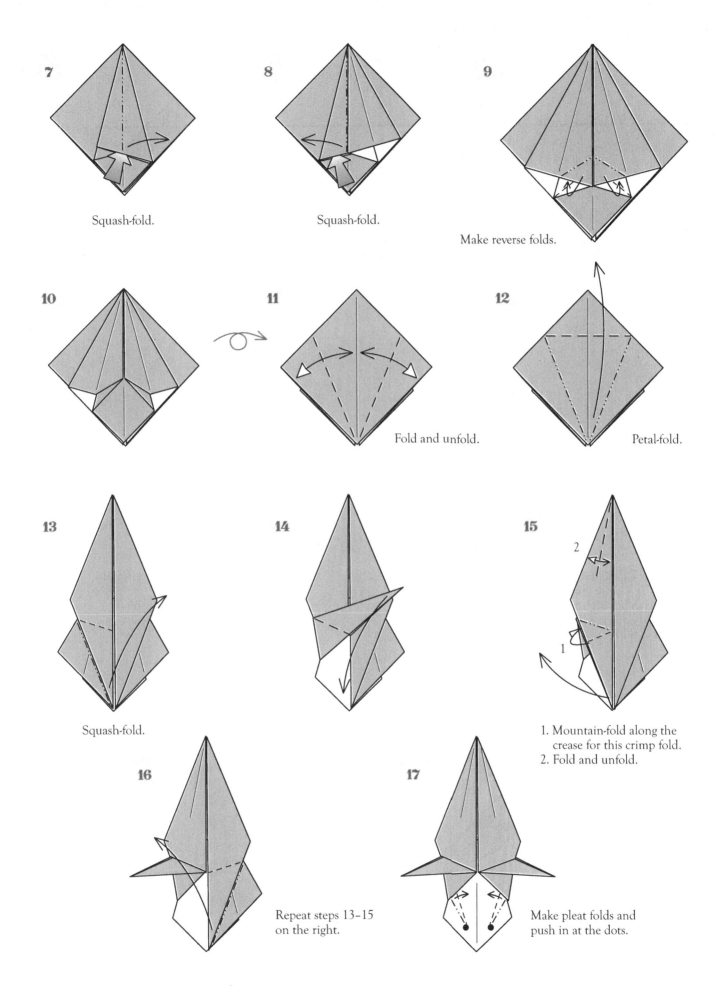

7

Squash-fold.

8

Squash-fold.

9

Make reverse folds.

10

11

Fold and unfold.

12

Petal-fold.

13

Squash-fold.

14

15

2

1

1. Mountain-fold along the crease for this crimp fold.
2. Fold and unfold.

16

Repeat steps 13–15 on the right.

17

Make pleat folds and push in at the dots.

18

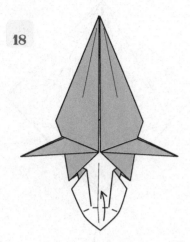

This is 3D. Flatten.

19

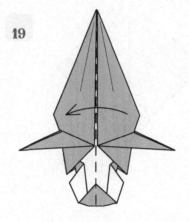

Fold in half and rotate.

20

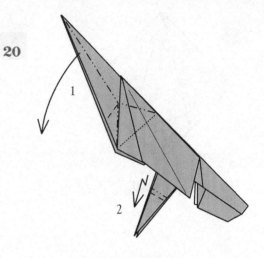

1. Double-rabbit-ear.
2. Crimp-fold, repeat behind.

21

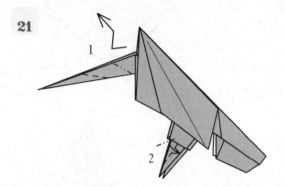

1. Make reverse folds.
2. Reverse-fold the top layer,
   repeat on the other side
   and repeat behind.

22

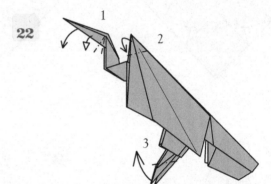

1. Outside-reverse-fold and spread.
2. Reverse-fold.
3. Reverse-fold, repeat behind.

23

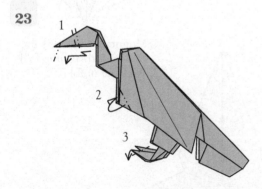

1. Crimp-fold and reverse-fold.
2. Repeat behind.
3. Reverse-fold, repeat behind.

24

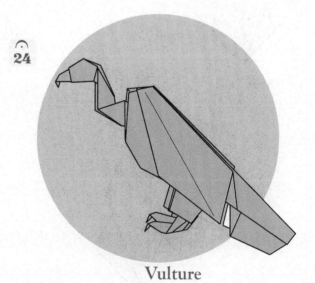

Vulture

Flamingo

Found in large groups, flamingos live by salt lakes, swamps, and sandy islands. A group of flamingos is a flamboyance. They dine on algae, shrimp and other small crustaceans, which gives them their distinct pink feathers. They make simple nests from mud. Long legs allow them to wade deeper in water than most birds. To fly, they begin by running in the direction of the wind.

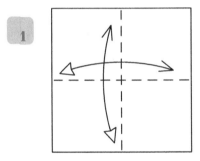

Fold and unfold.

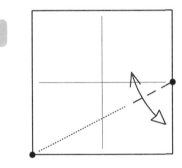

Fold and unfold.

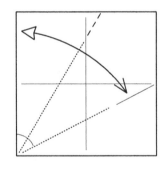

Biesect the angle. Fold and unfold at the top.

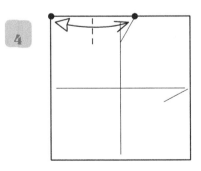

Fold and unfold.

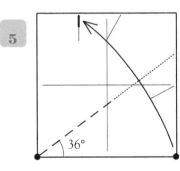

Bring the corner to the line. The angle is exactly 36°.

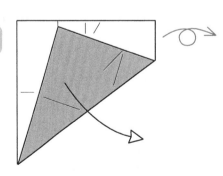

Unfold.

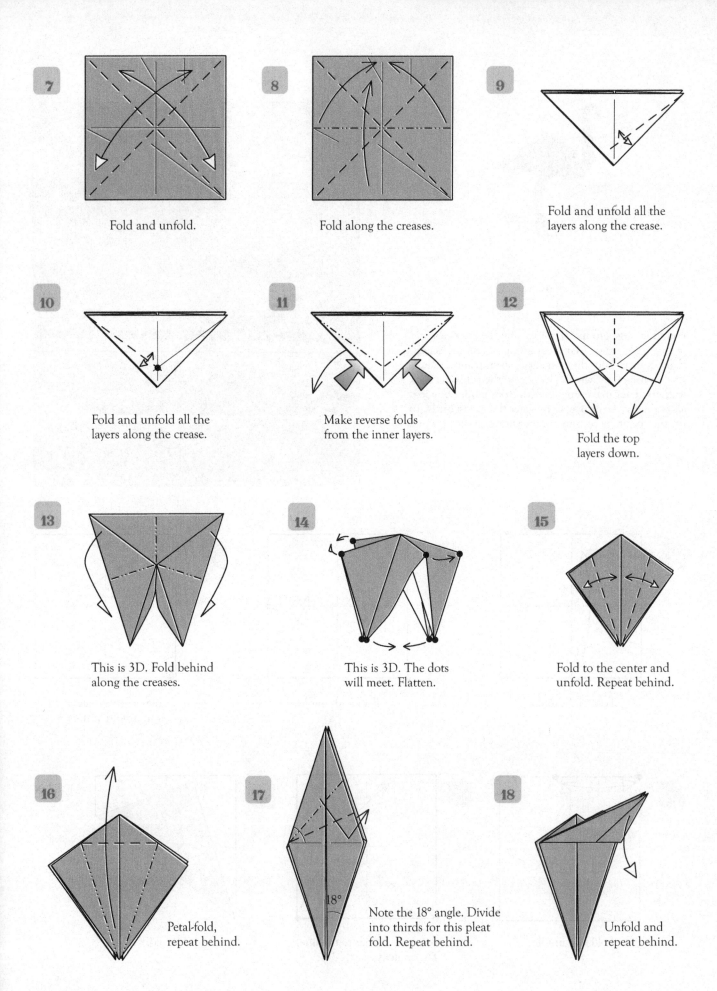

7 Fold and unfold.

8 Fold along the creases.

9 Fold and unfold all the layers along the crease.

10 Fold and unfold all the layers along the crease.

11 Make reverse folds from the inner layers.

12 Fold the top layers down.

13 This is 3D. Fold behind along the creases.

14 This is 3D. The dots will meet. Flatten.

15 Fold to the center and unfold. Repeat behind.

16 Petal-fold, repeat behind.

17 Note the 18° angle. Divide into thirds for this pleat fold. Repeat behind.

18°

18 Unfold and repeat behind.

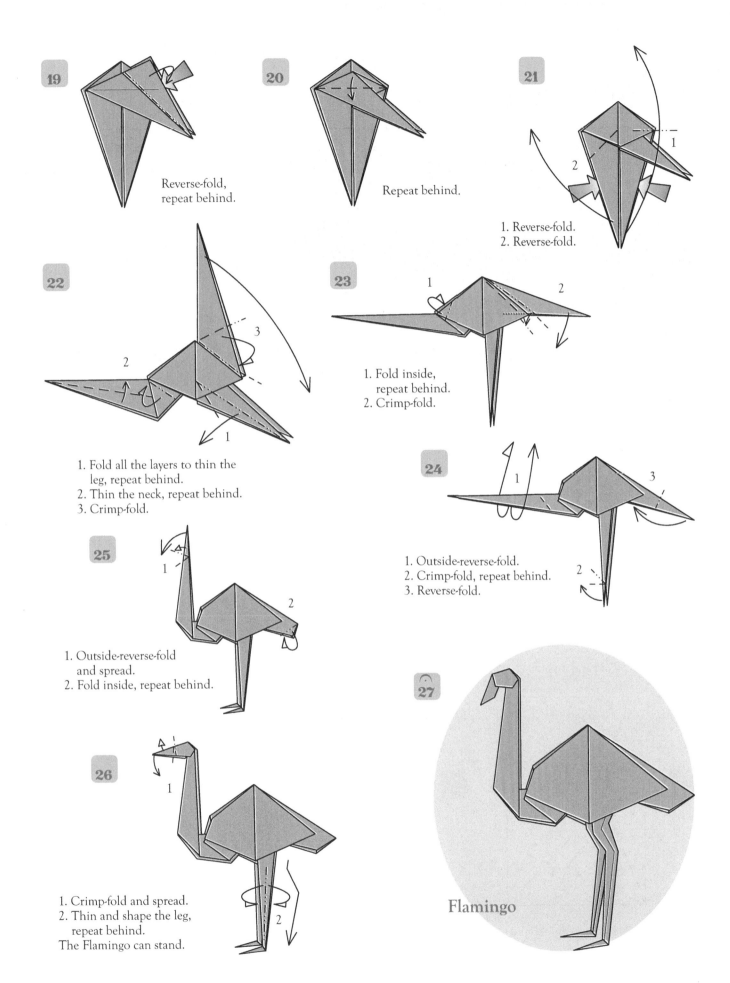

19

Reverse-fold,
repeat behind.

20

Repeat behind.

21

1. Reverse-fold.
2. Reverse-fold.

22

1. Fold all the layers to thin the
   leg, repeat behind.
2. Thin the neck, repeat behind.
3. Crimp-fold.

23

1. Fold inside,
   repeat behind.
2. Crimp-fold.

24

1. Outside-reverse-fold.
2. Crimp-fold, repeat behind.
3. Reverse-fold.

25

1. Outside-reverse-fold
   and spread.
2. Fold inside, repeat behind.

26

1. Crimp-fold and spread.
2. Thin and shape the leg,
   repeat behind.
The Flamingo can stand.

27

Flamingo

Black-backed Puffback

The black-backed puffback is a 7 inch long bird from Africa south of the equator. They spend much of their time in tree tops in wooded areas. Their distinct red eyes contrast with their black and white feathers. Highly active in search of food, they dine on caterpillars, ants, termites, beetles and fruit.

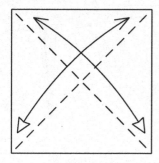

Fold and unfold.

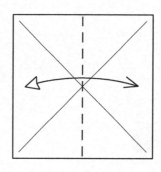

Fold and unfold.

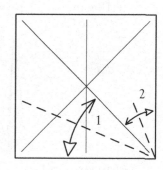

Fold and unfold at 1 and 2.

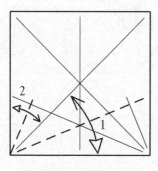

Fold and unfold at 1 and 2.

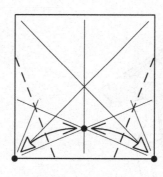

Fold and unfold.

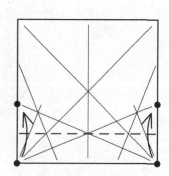

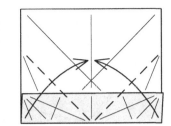

Fold to the center.

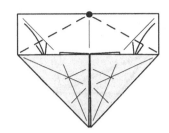

Tuck inside.

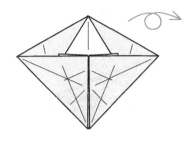

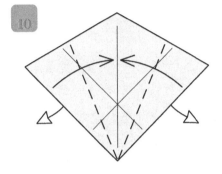

Fold to the center and
swing out from behind.

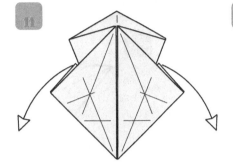

Pull out.

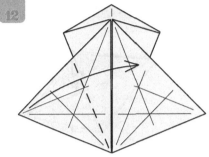

Fold along the crease.

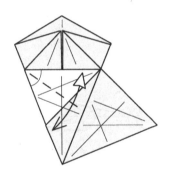

Fold and unfold.

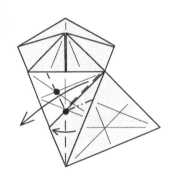

This is similar
to a rabbit ear.

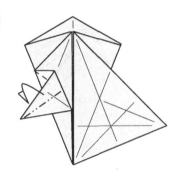

Tuck inside.

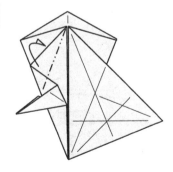

Fold along the crease.

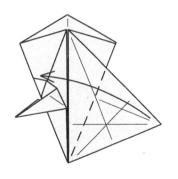

Repeat steps 12–16
on the right.

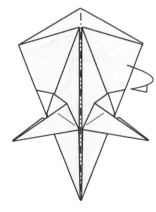

Fold in half and rotate.

Black-backed Puffback **49**

19

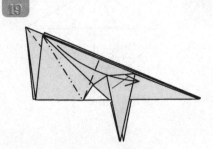

Squash-fold and
repeat behind.

20

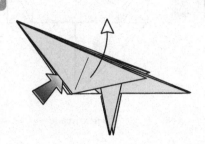

Unlock and pull out the
paper. Repeat behind.

21

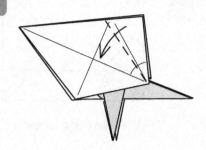

Repeat behind.

22

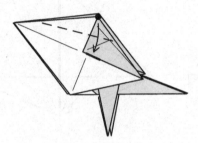

The dot will meet the
bold line. Repeat behind.

23

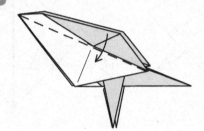

Repeat behind.

24

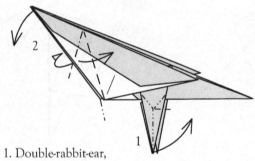

1. Double-rabbit-ear,
   repeat behind.
2. Crimp-fold.

25

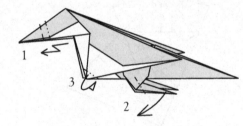

1. Crimp-fold.
2. Reverse-fold, repeat behind.
3. Fold inside, repeat behind.

26

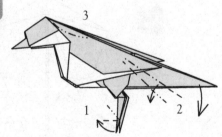

1. Crimp-fold, repeat behind.
2. Crimp-fold.
3. Shape the head.

27

**Black-backed
Puffback**

Hornbill

The hornbill has a large, heavy bill which is adept at catching insects, reptiles, and other small animals. They especially like figs and can eat over 100 in a meal. They cohabitation well with other animals and will help monkeys by eating the insects that annoy them. They live in flocks in grasslands and tropical forests. Unlike most birds, they have large eyelashes made of feathers.

1

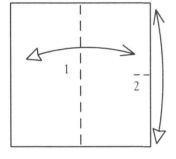

1. Fold and unfold.
2. Fold and unfold on the edge.

2

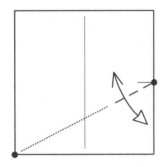

Fold and unfold.

3

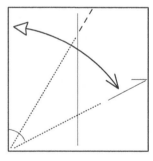

Bisect the angle. Fold and unfold at the top.

4

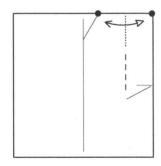

Fold and unfold.

5

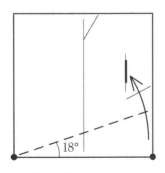

Bring the corner to the line to form 18°.

6

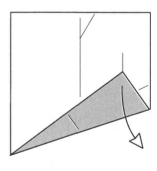

Unfold.

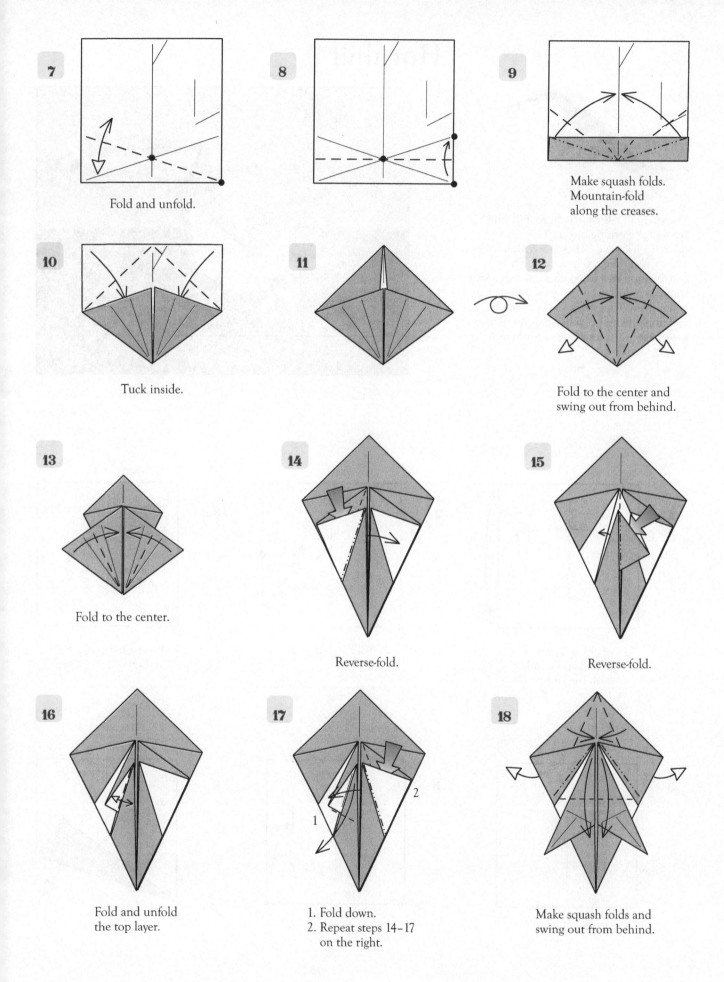

7

Fold and unfold.

8

9

Make squash folds.
Mountain-fold
along the creases.

10

Tuck inside.

11

12

Fold to the center and
swing out from behind.

13

Fold to the center.

14

Reverse-fold.

15

Reverse-fold.

16

Fold and unfold
the top layer.

17

1. Fold down.
2. Repeat steps 14–17
   on the right.

18

Make squash folds and
swing out from behind.

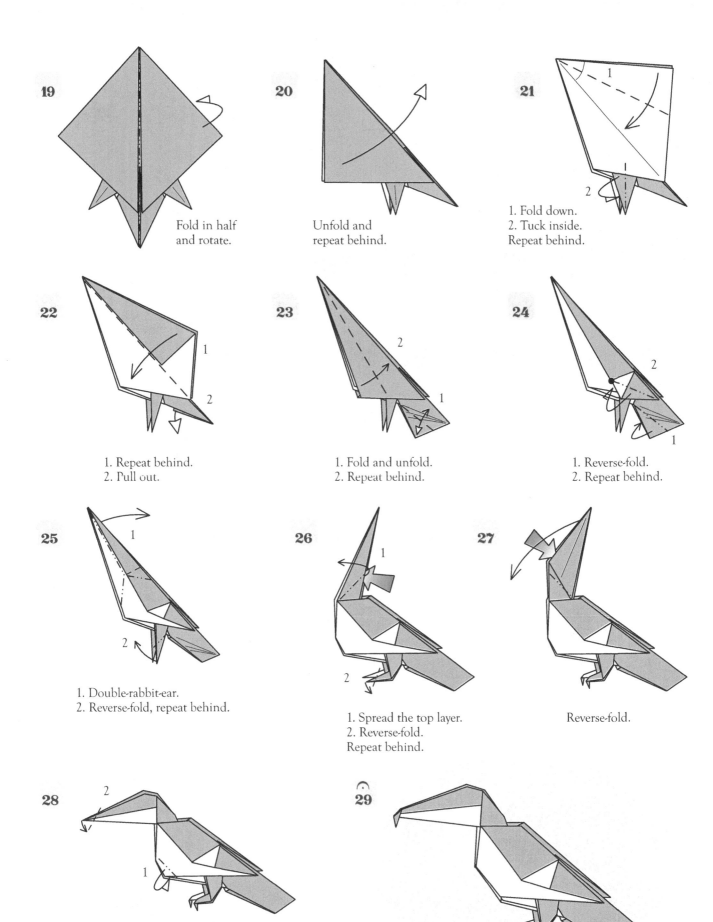

19 Fold in half and rotate.

20 Unfold and repeat behind.

21
1. Fold down.
2. Tuck inside.
Repeat behind.

22
1. Repeat behind.
2. Pull out.

23
1. Fold and unfold.
2. Repeat behind.

24
1. Reverse-fold.
2. Repeat behind.

25
1. Double-rabbit-ear.
2. Reverse-fold, repeat behind.

26
1. Spread the top layer.
2. Reverse-fold.
Repeat behind.

27 Reverse-fold.

28
1. Repeat behind.
2. Outside-reverse-fold.

29

Hornbill

Hoopoe

The hoopoe has a beautiful crown of feathers that can be raised or lowered when they are calm. Feeding on berries, insects and other small animals, they use their long bill to probe for food on the ground. They can catch insects while in flight. Unlike most birds, they do not build nests, but use holes in trees or crevices on cliffs. Just like a skunk, they can spray a strong odor toward a predator when threatened.

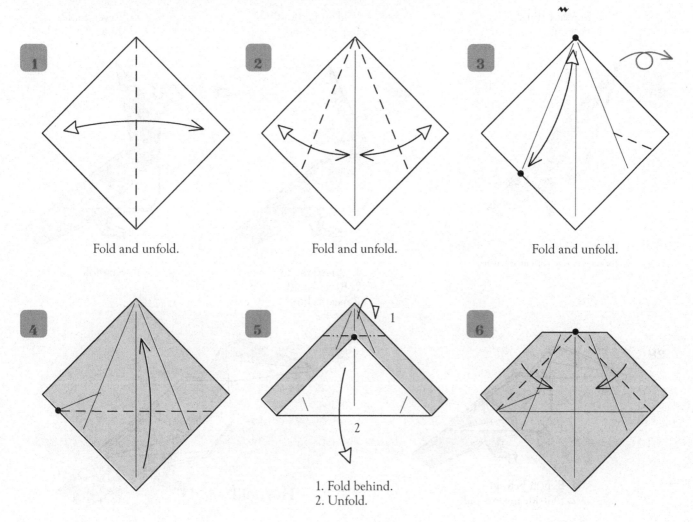

1 Fold and unfold.

2 Fold and unfold.

3 Fold and unfold.

4

5
1. Fold behind.
2. Unfold.

6

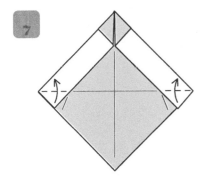

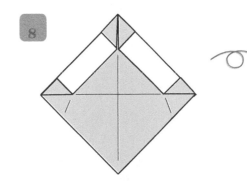

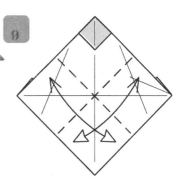

Fold and unfold.

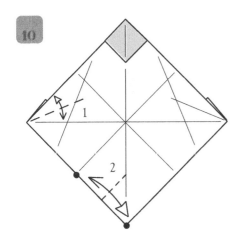

Fold and unfold
at 1 and 2.

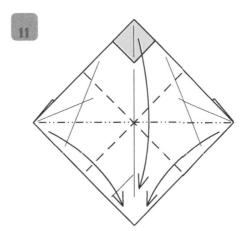

Fold along the creases.

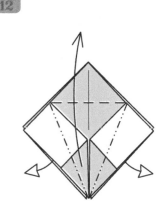

Petal-fold and swing
out from behind.

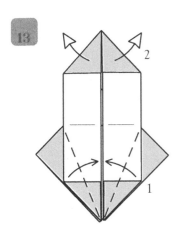

1. Fold to the center.
2. Pull out.

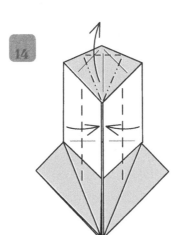

Petal-fold.

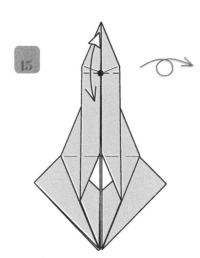

Fold and unfold.

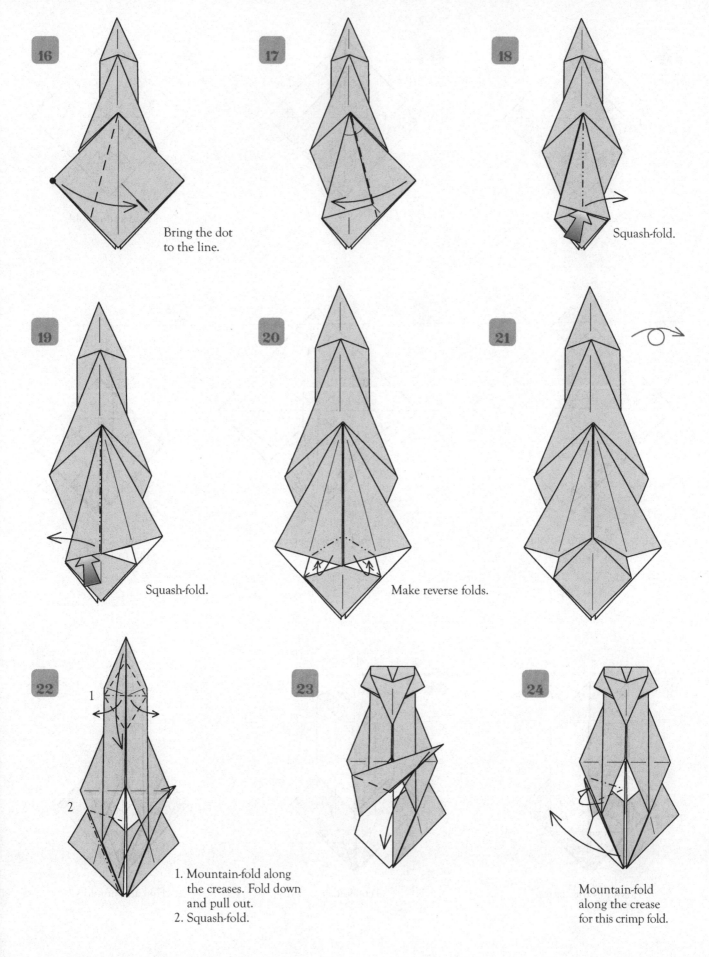

16 Bring the dot to the line.

17

18 Squash-fold.

19 Squash-fold.

20 Make reverse folds.

21

22
1. Mountain-fold along the creases. Fold down and pull out.
2. Squash-fold.

23

24 Mountain-fold along the crease for this crimp fold.

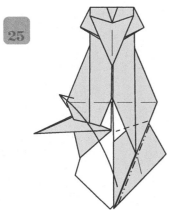

25

Repeat steps 22–24
on the right.

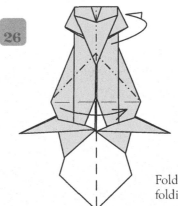

26

Fold in half while
folding the head up.

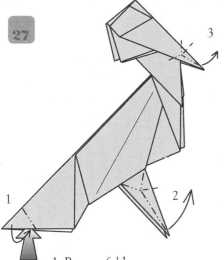

27

3

2

1

1. Reverse-fold.
2. Double-rabbit-ear,
   repeat behind.
3. Double-rabbit-ear.

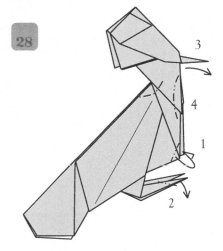

28

3

4

1

2

1. Fold inside, repeat behind.
2. Reverse-fold, repeat behind.
3. Curl the beak.
4. Shape the neck.

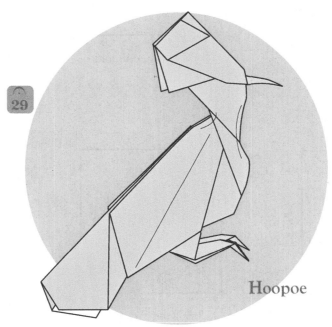

29

Hoopoe

Stork

Storks are large wading birds with large bills. Feeding by shallow water, they hunt for fish, insects and other small animals, They build nests in trees, building and other made-made structures, and among rocks. Each year, they add to their nests as they become larger. They soar when flying by following thermal air currents.

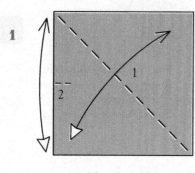

1. Fold and unfold.
2. Fold and unfold on the edge.

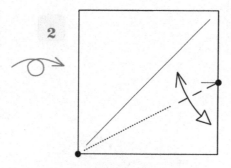

Fold and unfold.

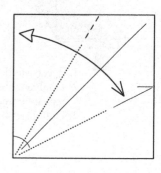

Biesect the angle. Fold and unfold at the top.

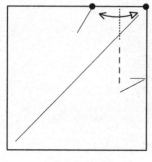

Fold and unfold.

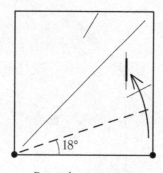

Bring the corner to the line to form 18°.

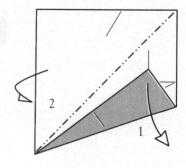

1. Unfold.
2. Fold behind.

7

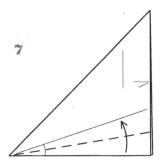

Repeat behind.

8

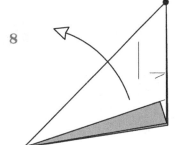

Unfold and rotate the dot to the bottom.

9

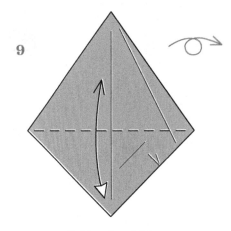

Fold and unfold.

10

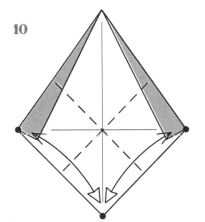

Fold and unfold.

11

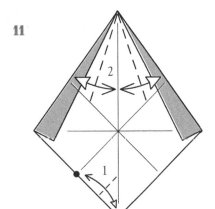

1. Fold and unfold.
2. Fold to the center and unfold.

12

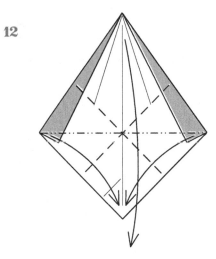

Fold along the creases.

13

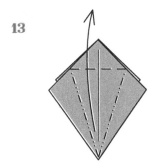

Mountain-fold along the creases for this petal fold.

14

Fold to the center and unfold.

15

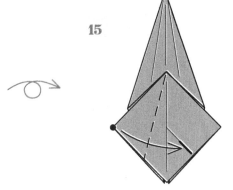

Bring the dot to the line.

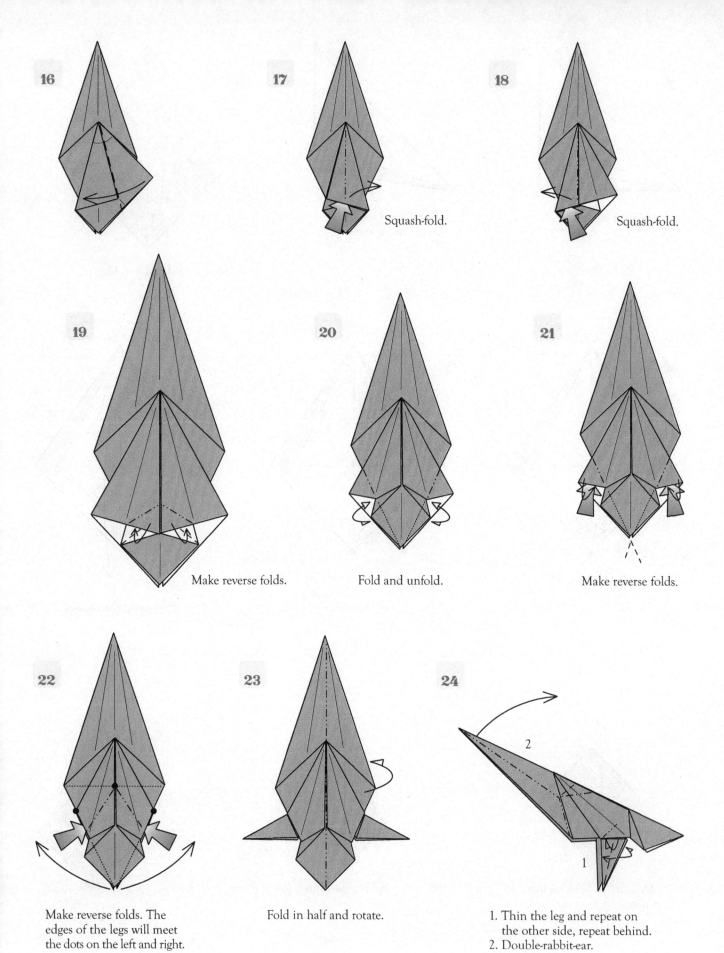

16

17 Squash-fold.

18 Squash-fold.

19 Make reverse folds.

20 Fold and unfold.

21 Make reverse folds.

22 Make reverse folds. The edges of the legs will meet the dots on the left and right.

23 Fold in half and rotate.

24
1. Thin the leg and repeat on the other side, repeat behind.
2. Double-rabbit-ear.

25

1. Reverse-fold.
2. Reverse-fold.

26

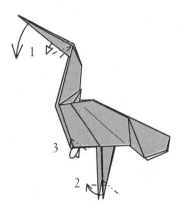

1. Outside-reverse-fold and spread.
2. Crimp-fold, repeat behind.
3. Fold inside, repeat behind.

27

1. Crimp-fold.
2. Crimp-fold.
3. Thin the leg, repeat behind.

28

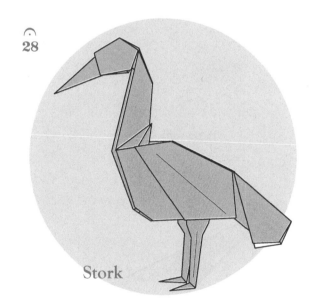

Stork

Ostrich

As the largest bird, the ostrich is 9 feet tall. Though flightless, it is the fastest of any two-legged animal, and can run at speeds of 45 miles an hour. Their eyes are the largest of any land animal. Thriving in African savannas and open woodlands, they feed on plants, snakes and rodents. Their strong legs can kick so powerfully that it could injure a lion.

Begin with step 24 of the Stork (page 58).

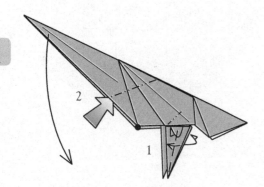

1. Thin the leg and repeat on the other side, repeat behind.
2. Reverse-fold so the edge meets the dot.

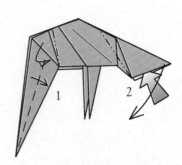

1. Reverse-fold, repeat behind.
2. Reverse-fold.

3

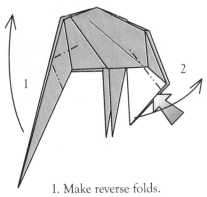

1. Make reverse folds.
2. Reverse-fold.

4

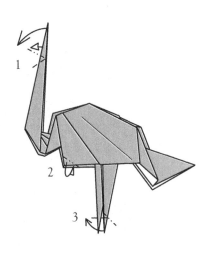

1. Outside-reverse-fold and spread the head.
2. Fold inside, repeat behind.
3. Crimp-fold, repeat behind.

5

1. Crimp-fold.
2. Reverse-fold.
3. Thin and shape the legs, repeat behind.

6

Ostrich

Toucan

Found in rainforest canopies, toucans spend most of their time sitting high in trees. They are the noisiest of birds. With short wings, they only fly for short distances and need to flap them a lot. The large, colorful bills allow them to gather food in trees, from fruits and nuts to insects. They will also eat fish and other small animals. The large bills are light-weight but appear threatening to predators.

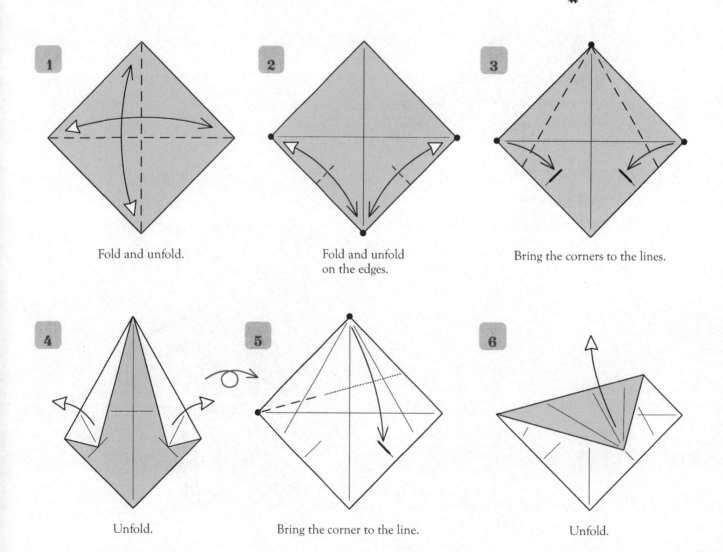

1 Fold and unfold.

2 Fold and unfold on the edges.

3 Bring the corners to the lines.

4 Unfold.

5 Bring the corner to the line.

6 Unfold.

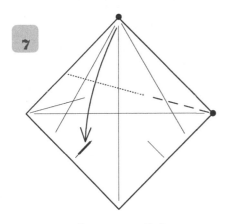

7

Repeat steps 5–6
on the right.

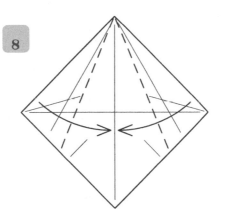

8

Fold to the center.

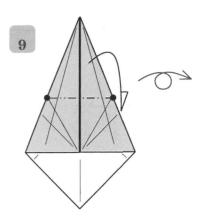

9

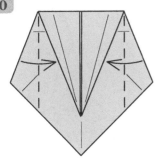

10

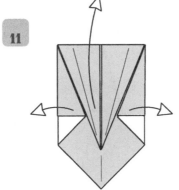

11

Unfold.

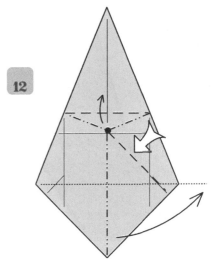

12

Lift up at the dot so the edges
meet at the dotted line.

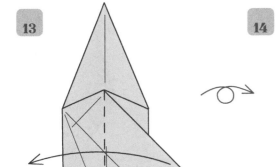

13

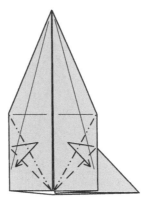

14

Make crimp folds
along the creases.

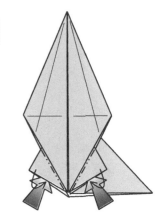

15

Make reverse folds.

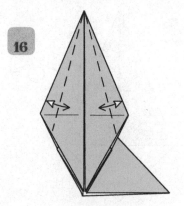

16

Fold and unfold along the creases.

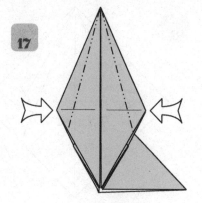

17

Spread at the bottom to sink.

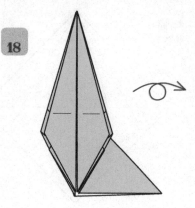

18

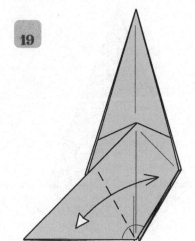

19

Fold and unfold.

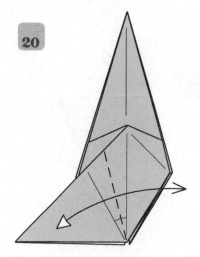

20

Fold and unfold.

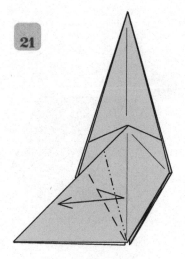

21

Crimp-fold along the creases.

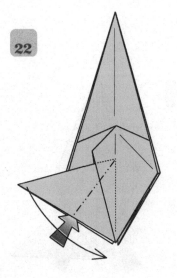

22

Reverse-fold.

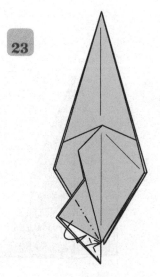

23

Reverse-fold and repeat behind.

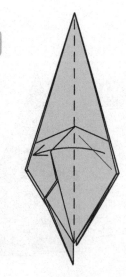

24

Fold in half and rotate.

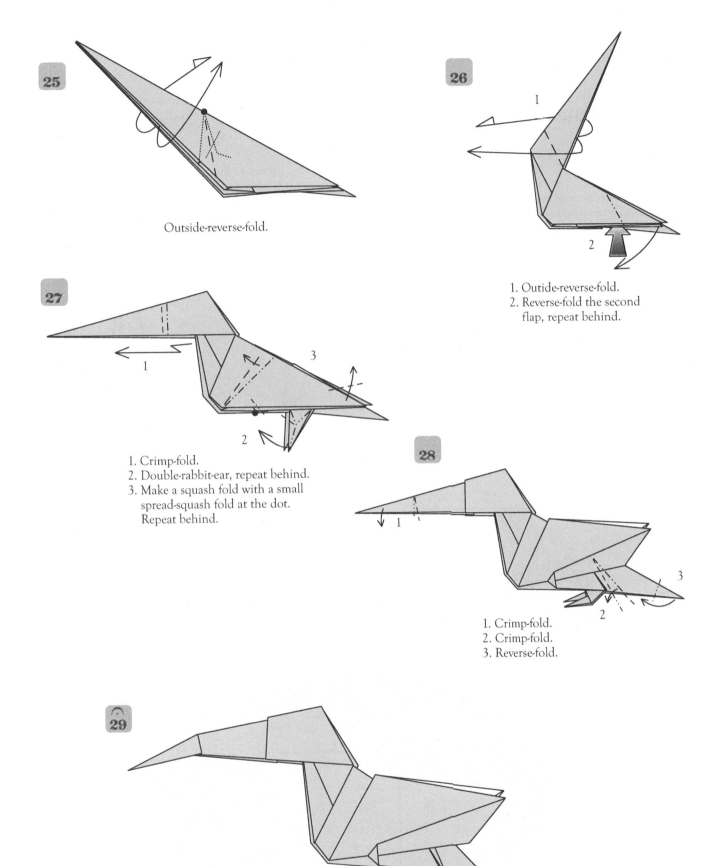

25

Outside-reverse-fold.

26

1
2

1. Outide-reverse-fold.
2. Reverse-fold the second
   flap, repeat behind.

27

1
2
3

1. Crimp-fold.
2. Double-rabbit-ear, repeat behind.
3. Make a squash fold with a small
   spread-squash fold at the dot.
   Repeat behind.

28

1
2
3

1. Crimp-fold.
2. Crimp-fold.
3. Reverse-fold.

29

Toucan

Third Movement

Minuet of Triangular Pyramids with a Trio of Spherical Gems

The minuet of Triangular Pyramids of varying heights and angles takes us back to the ground. Single sheet origami polyhedra represent the geometric and magical side of origami. From the low Mound through the Tetrahedron and ending at the tall Spire, these seven pyramids add interesting background to any scene. Each model has an equilateral triangular base.

Mound

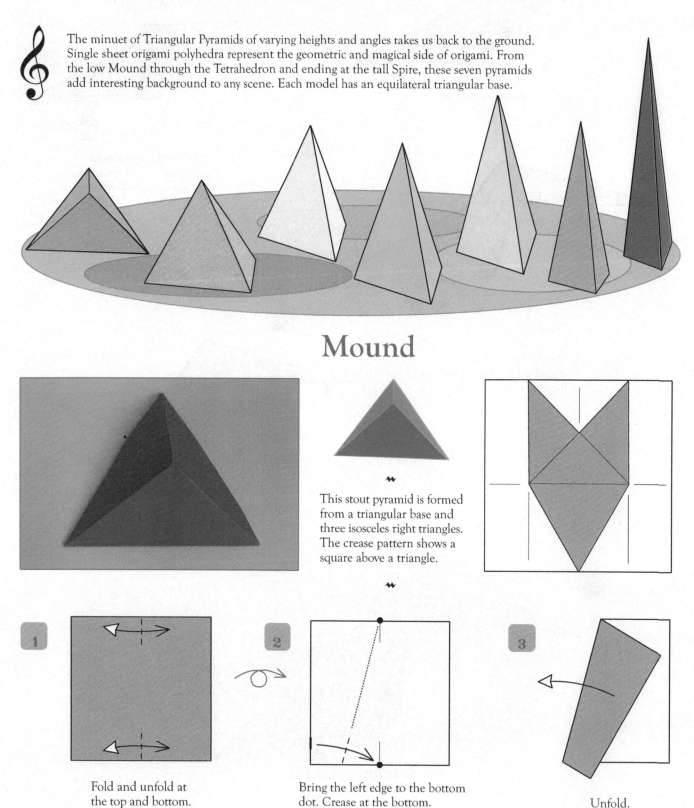

This stout pyramid is formed from a triangular base and three isosceles right triangles. The crease pattern shows a square above a triangle.

1 Fold and unfold at the top and bottom.

2 Bring the left edge to the bottom dot. Crease at the bottom.

3 Unfold.

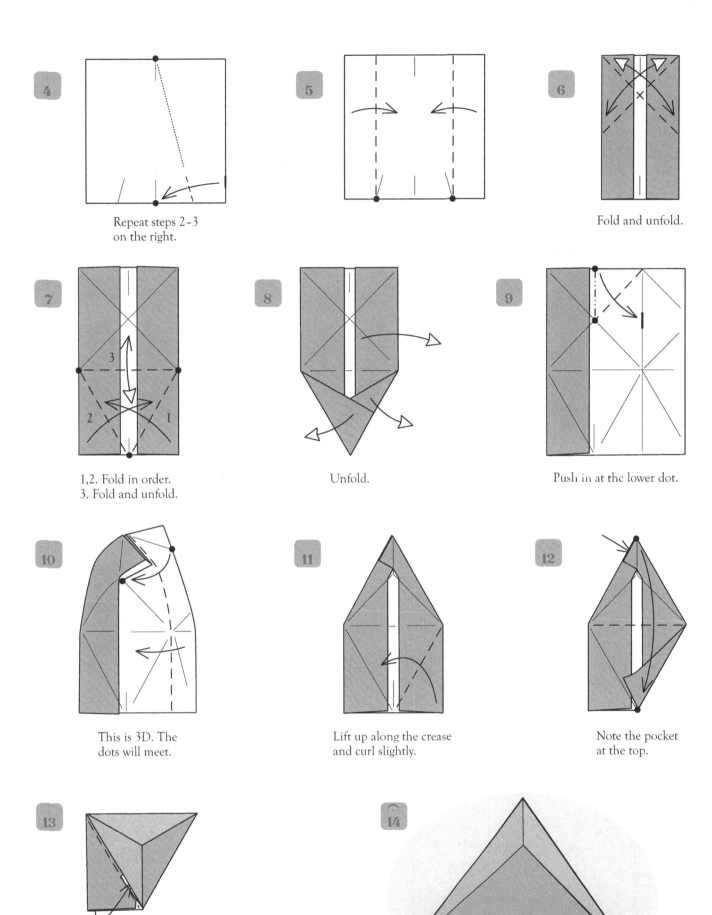

4 Repeat steps 2–3 on the right.

5

6 Fold and unfold.

7 1,2. Fold in order.
3. Fold and unfold.

8 Unfold.

9 Push in at the lower dot.

10 This is 3D. The dots will meet.

11 Lift up along the crease and curl slightly.

12 Note the pocket at the top.

13 Tuck inside the pocket.

14 Mound

Tetrahedron

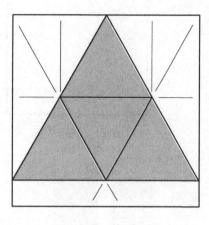

Composed of four equilateral triangles, this is the simplest of the five Platonic solids. Plato believed the tetrahedron represented fire because of its sharpness and simplicity.

1

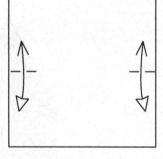

Fold and unfold on the left and right.

2

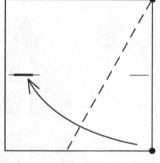

Bring the dot to the line.

3

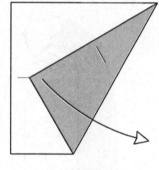

Unfold.

4

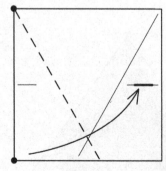

Repeat steps 2–3 in the opposite direction.

5

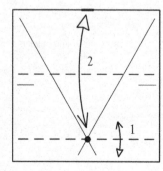

Fold and unfold at 1 and 2.

6

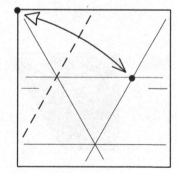

Fold and unfold.

7

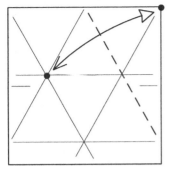

Fold and unfold.

8

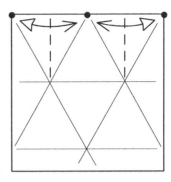

Fold and unfold.

9

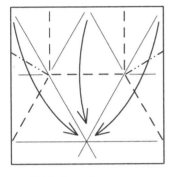

Fold along the creases.

10

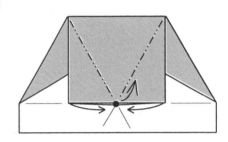

Lift up at the dot.

11

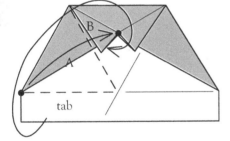

A will cover B and the tab
will wrap around inside.

12

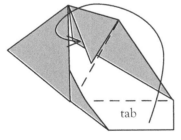

Repeat step 11
on the right.

13

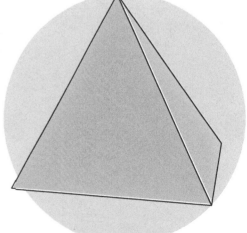

Tetrahedron

Crown

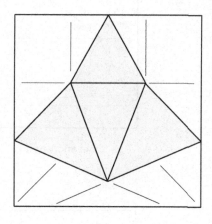

This pyramid is formed from a triangular base and three isosceles triangles, with an apex angle of 45°.

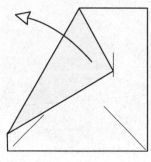

1 Fold and unfold at 1, 2, and 3.

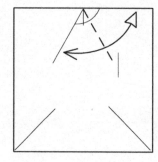

2 Fold and unfold.

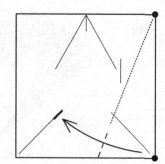

3 Bring the upper left corner to the line.

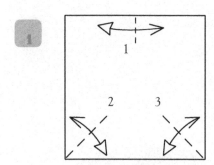

4 Unfold.

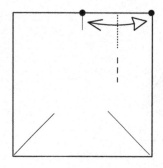

5 Fold and unfold.

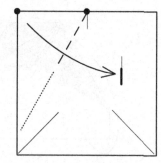

6 Bring the lower right corner to the line.

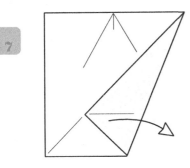

7

Unfold.

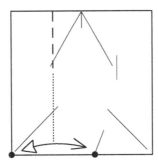

8

Fold and unfold
on the top.

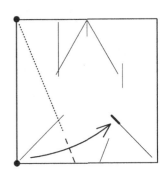

9

Repeat steps 6–8 in
the opposite direction.

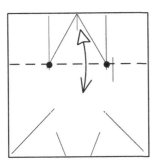

10

Fold and unfold.

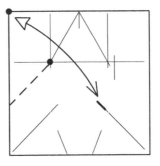

11

Fold and unfold.

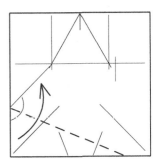

12

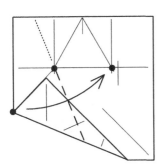

13

The dots will meet.

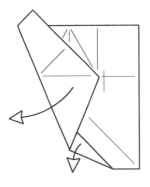

14

Unfold.

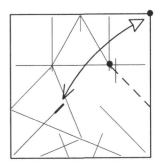

15

Repeat steps 11–14 in
the opposite direction.

Crown **73**

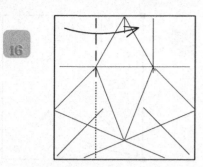

16 Fold along the crease.

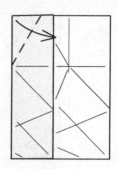

17 Fold along a hidden crease.

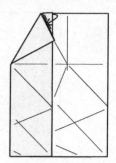

18 Tuck inside.

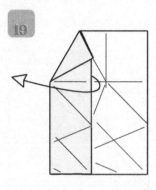

19 Open.

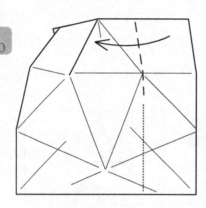

20 This is 3D. Repeat steps 16–19 on the right.

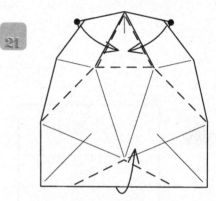

21 Fold along the creases. The dots will meet. Fold up at the bottom.

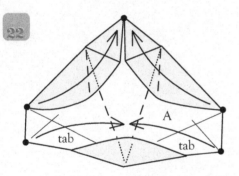

22 The three upper dots will meet and the bottom two dots will meet. Rotate to view A and the tab next to A, on the color side of the paper.

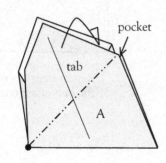

23 Tuck the tab into the center pocket. Repeat behind and rotate the dot to the top.

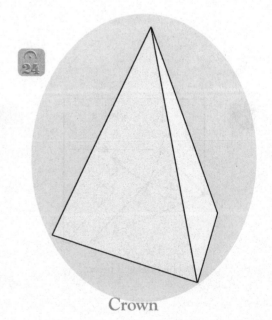

24 Crown

Pinnacle

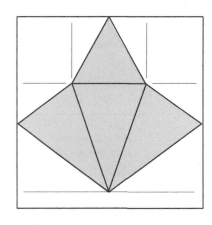

This pyramid is formed from a triangular base and three isosceles triangles, with an apex angle of 36°.

1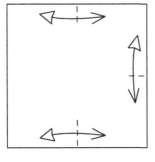

Fold and unfold.

2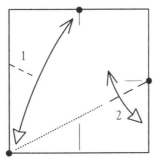

Fold and unfold at 1 and 2.

3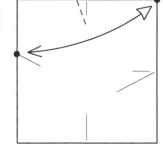

Fold and unfold.

4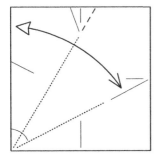

Biesect the angle. Fold and unfold at the top.

5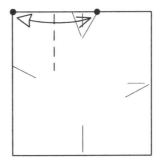

Fold and unfold.

6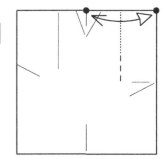

Fold and unfold.

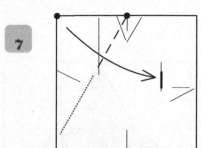

7 Bring the upper left corner to the line.

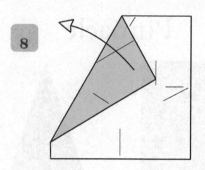

8 Unfold.

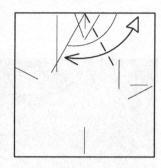

9 Fold and unfold.

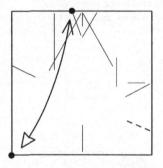

10 Fold and unfold on the right.

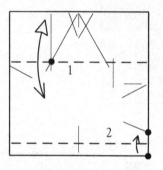

11
1. Fold and unfold.
2. Fold up.

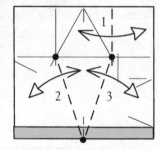

12 Fold and unfold at 1, 2, and 3.

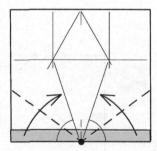

13

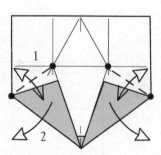

14
1. Fold and unfold.
2. Unfold.

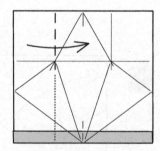

15 Fold along the crease.

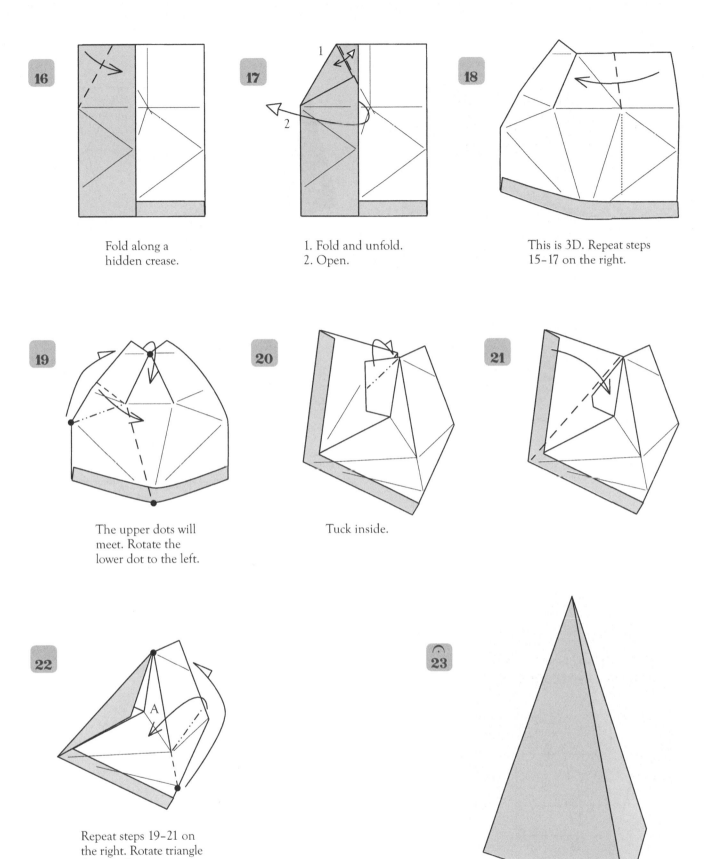

16 Fold along a hidden crease.

17 1. Fold and unfold. 2. Open.

18 This is 3D. Repeat steps 15–17 on the right.

19 The upper dots will meet. Rotate the lower dot to the left.

20 Tuck inside.

21

22 Repeat steps 19–21 on the right. Rotate triangle A to the bottom.

23 Pinnacle

Peak

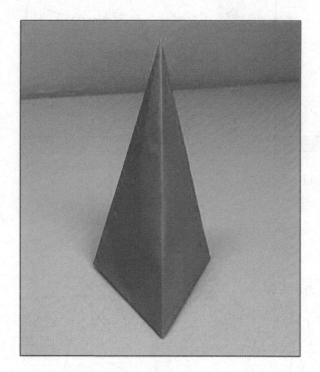

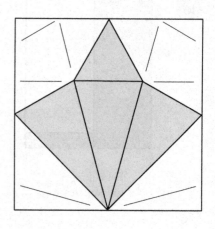

This tall pyramid is formed from a triangular base and three isosceles triangles, with an apex angle of 30°.

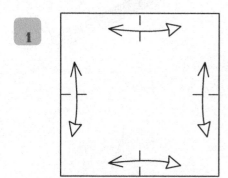

Fold and unfold to find the centers on each side.

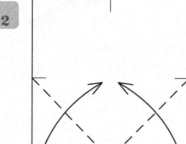

Fold the left edge to the dot.

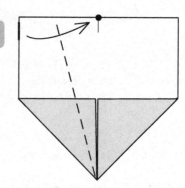

Fold and unfold.

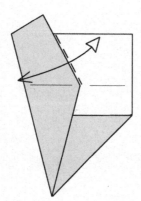

Fold and unfold.

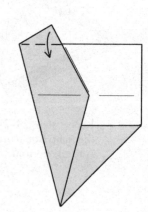

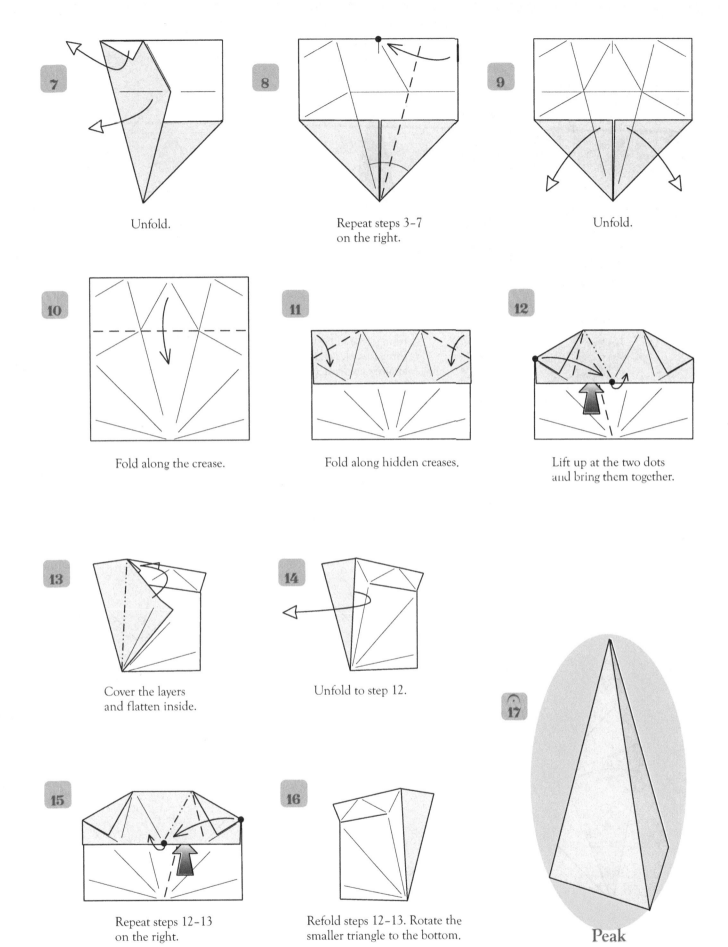

7 Unfold.

8 Repeat steps 3–7 on the right.

9 Unfold.

10 Fold along the crease.

11 Fold along hidden creases.

12 Lift up at the two dots and bring them together.

13 Cover the layers and flatten inside.

14 Unfold to step 12.

15 Repeat steps 12–13 on the right.

16 Refold steps 12–13. Rotate the smaller triangle to the bottom.

17

Peak

Pike

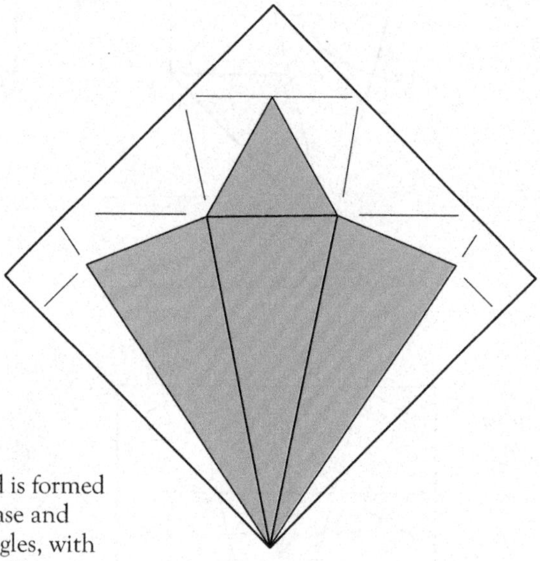

This pointy pyramid is formed from a triangular base and three isosceles triangles, with an apex angle of 22.5°.

1

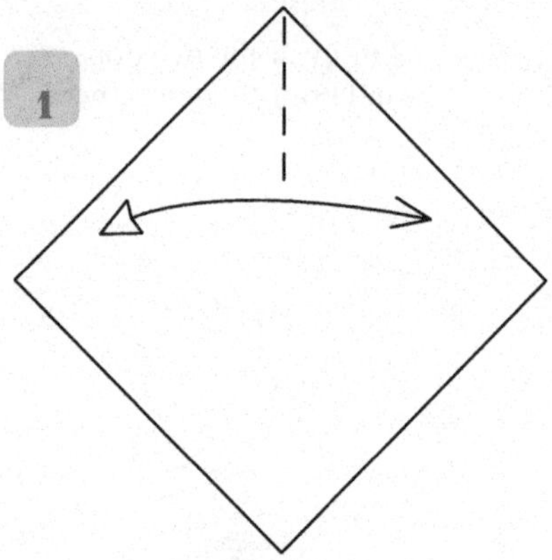

Fold and unfold at the top.

2

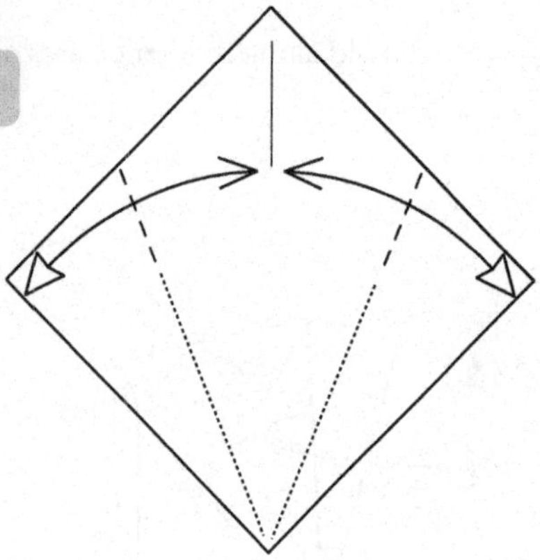

Fold to the center and unfold.

3

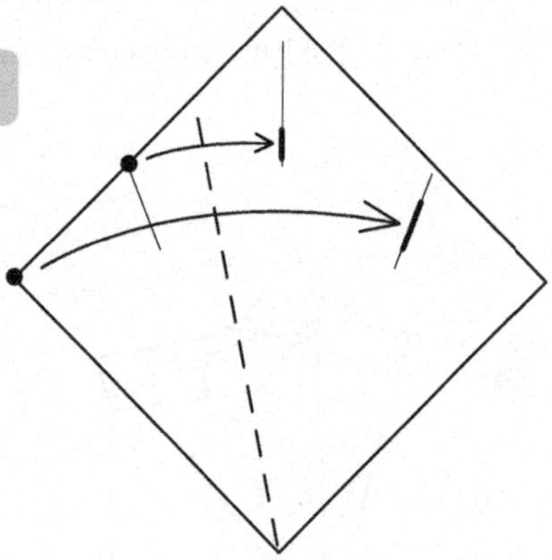

4

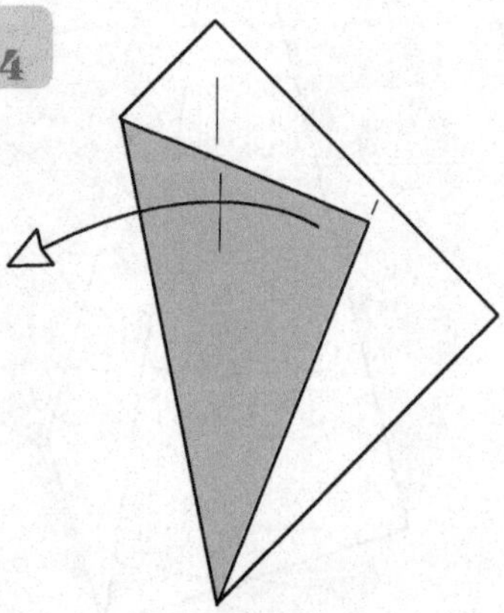

Unfold.

5

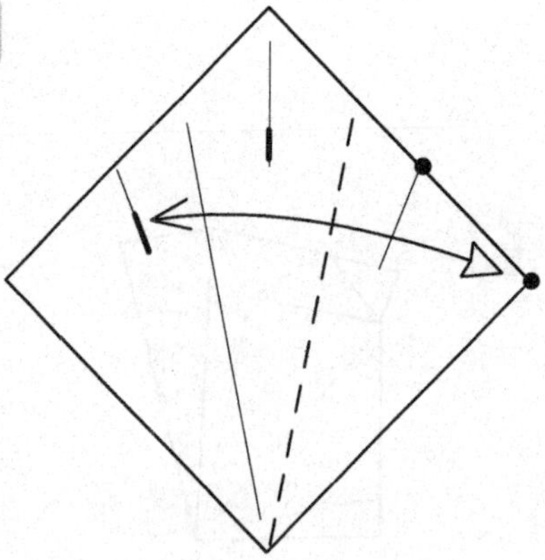

Fold and unfold.

6

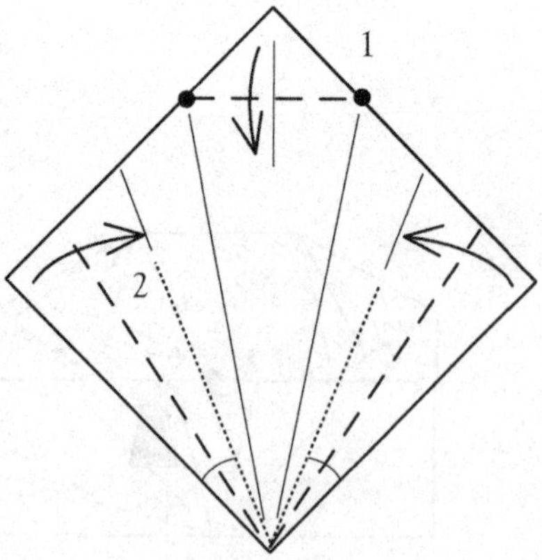

1. Fold down.
2. Bisect the angles.

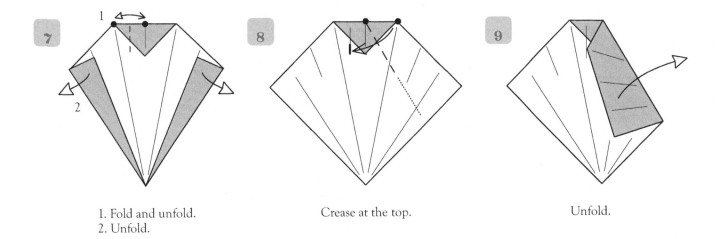

1. Fold and unfold.
2. Unfold.

Crease at the top.

Unfold.

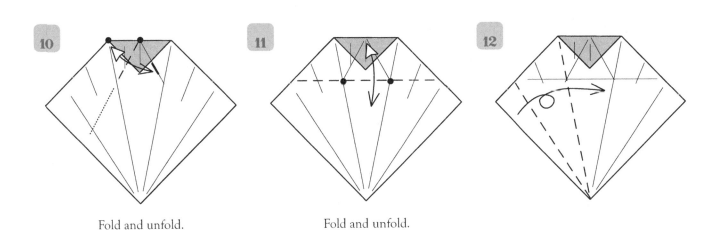

Fold and unfold.

Fold and unfold.

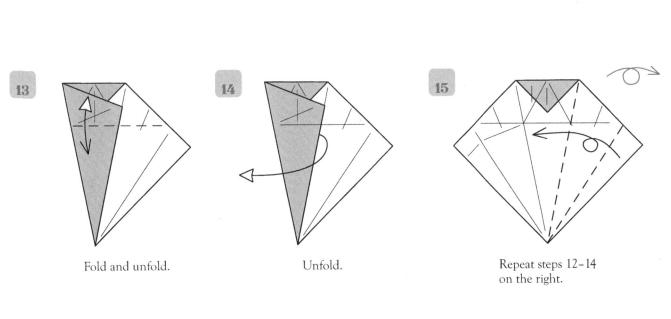

Fold and unfold.

Unfold.

Repeat steps 12–14
on the right.

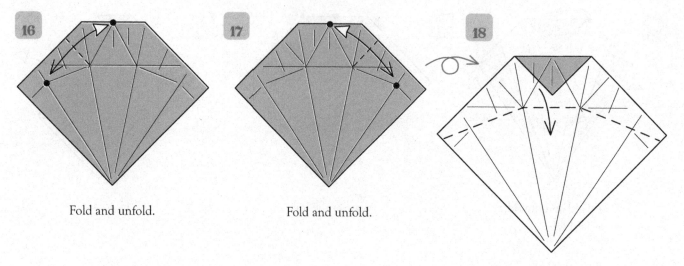

16 Fold and unfold.

17 Fold and unfold.

18 Fold along the creases.

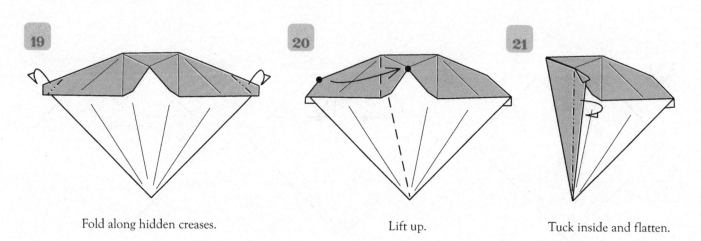

19 Fold along hidden creases.

20 Lift up.

21 Tuck inside and flatten.

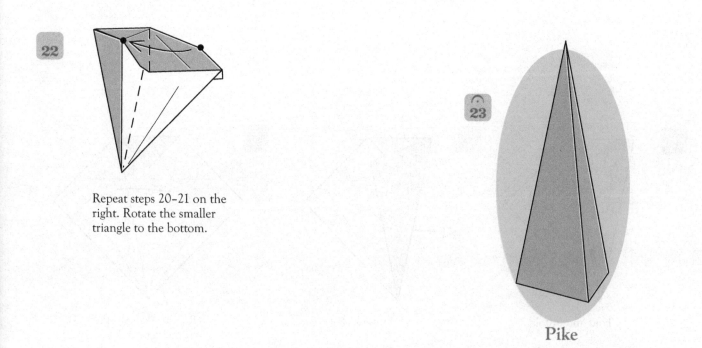

22 Repeat steps 20–21 on the right. Rotate the smaller triangle to the bottom.

23

Pike

Spire

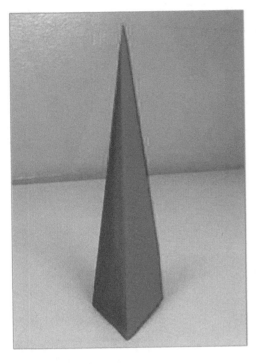

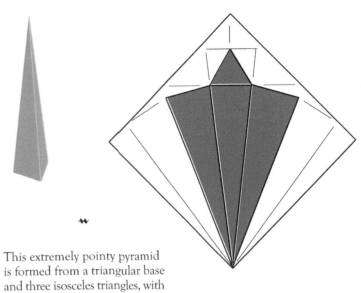

This extremely pointy pyramid is formed from a triangular base and three isosceles triangles, with an apex angle of 15°.

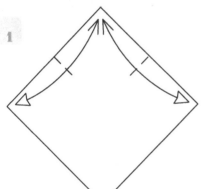

1 Fold and unfold in half on the edges.

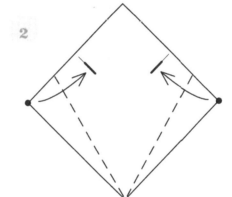

2 Bring the corners to the creases, folding near the top.

3 Fold to the edges.

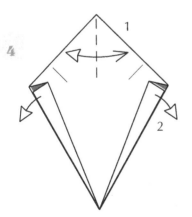

4
1. Fold and unfold.
2. Unfold.

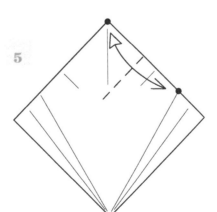

5 Fold and unfold.

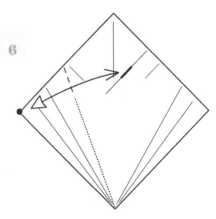

6 Fold and unfold the corner to the crease. Crease near the top.

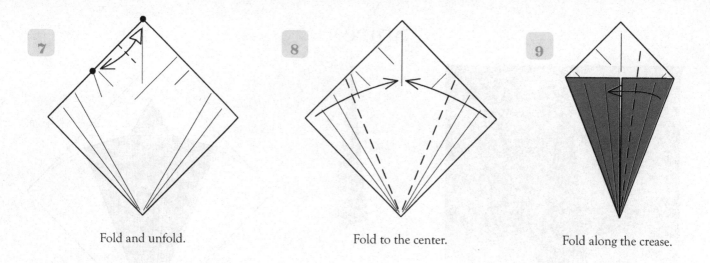

7 Fold and unfold.

8 Fold to the center.

9 Fold along the crease.

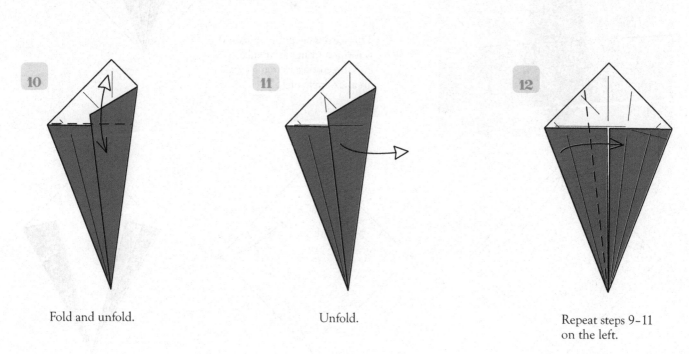

10 Fold and unfold.

11 Unfold.

12 Repeat steps 9–11 on the left.

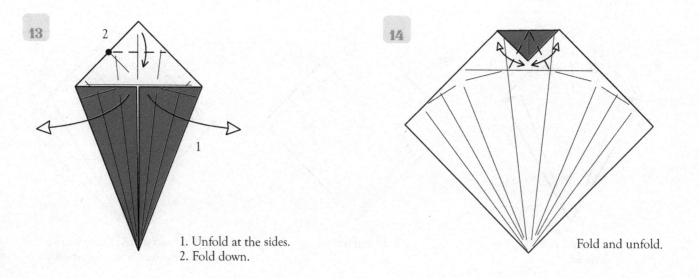

13
2
1

1. Unfold at the sides.
2. Fold down.

14 Fold and unfold.

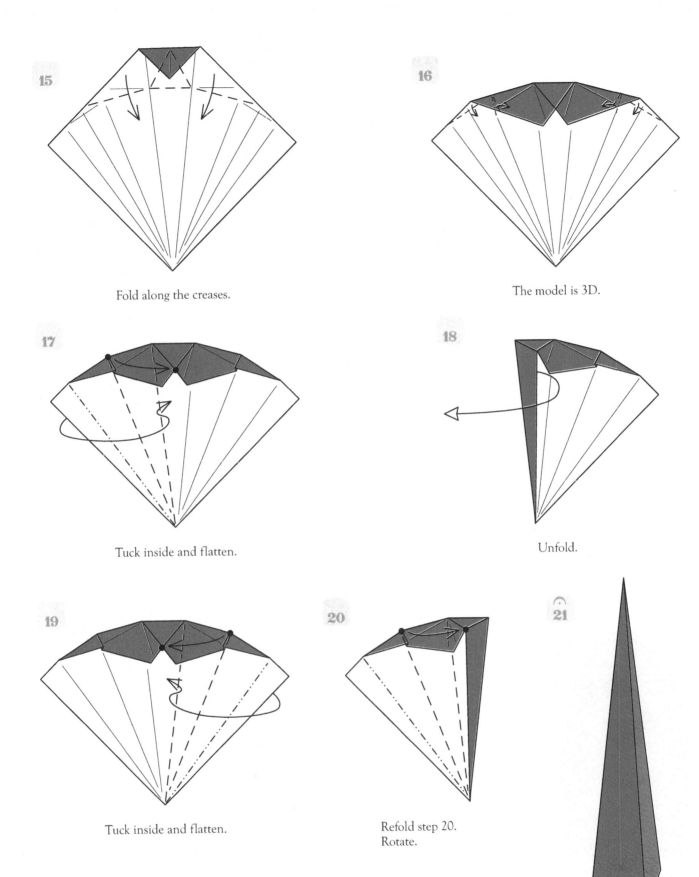

15 Fold along the creases.

16 The model is 3D.

17 Tuck inside and flatten.

18 Unfold.

19 Tuck inside and flatten.

20 Refold step 20.
Rotate.

21 Spire

Trio of Spherical Gems

The trio of Spherical Gems are found in the skies, as the minuet of Triangular Pyramids points to these. A twelve-sided Hexagonal Dipyramid inscribed in a sphere spins on its axis. The Jackstone lights up the sky. The Heptagon is shaped as an octahedron but alternate sides are sunken. Careful folding and skill allows these models to lock well at the completion of their folding sequence.

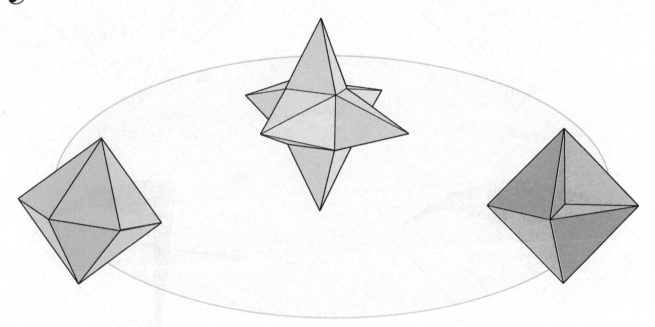

Hexagonal Dipyramid in a Sphere

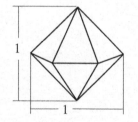

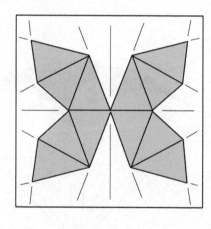

This dipyramid is inscribed in a sphere. The angles of each of the twelve triangles are 41.41°, 69.3°, and 69.3°. Because it is inscribed in a sphere, when viewed just right, it has the silhouette of a square. The landmarks in the early steps set up this version so all the angles will be exact. By step 5, the line folded is in the exact location.

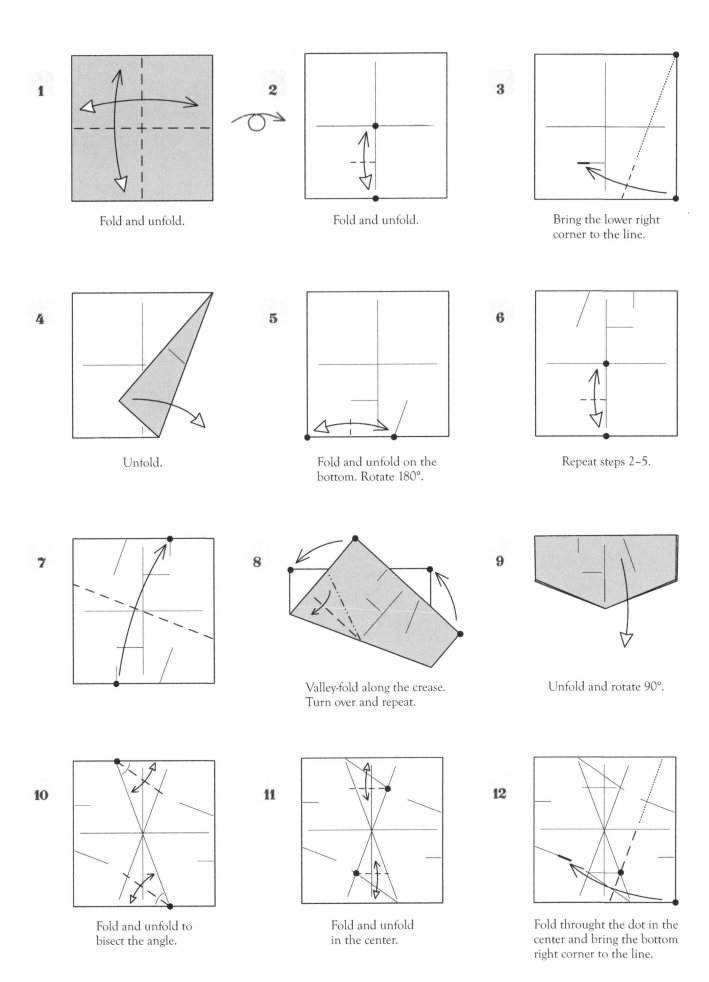

1 Fold and unfold.

2 Fold and unfold.

3 Bring the lower right corner to the line.

4 Unfold.

5 Fold and unfold on the bottom. Rotate 180°.

6 Repeat steps 2–5.

7

8 Valley-fold along the crease. Turn over and repeat.

9 Unfold and rotate 90°.

10 Fold and unfold to bisect the angle.

11 Fold and unfold in the center.

12 Fold throught the dot in the center and bring the bottom right corner to the line.

Hexagonal Dipyramid in a Sphere **87**

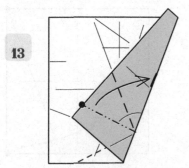

13

Valley-fold along a hidden crease and mountain-fold the dot to the right edge.

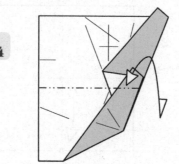

14

Fold and unfold all the layers along a partally hidden crease.

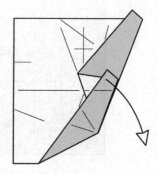

15

Unfold and rotate 180°.

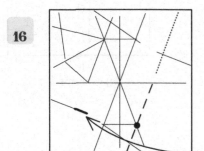

16

Repeat steps 12–15.

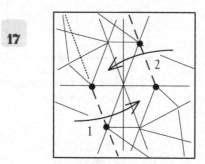

17

1. Repeat steps 12–15 on the left. Rotate 180°.
2. Repeat.

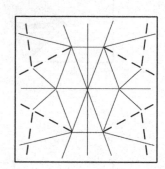

18

Fold and unfold along the creases.

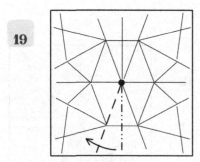

19

Push in at the dot.

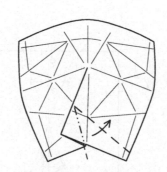

20

Valley-fold along the crease for this squash fold. Rotate 180°.

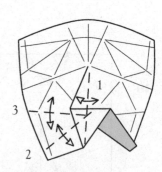

21

Fold and unfold along the creases. Rotate 180°.

22

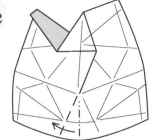

Repeat steps 19–21.
Then flatten.

23

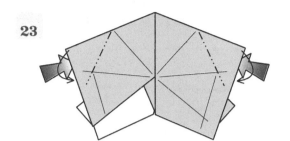

Reverse folds.

24

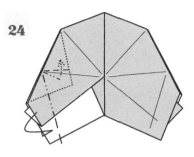

Fold the inside layers
together for this spine-lock
fold. Turn over and repeat.

25

Fold the edge to the dot.
Turn over and repeat.

26

1. Lift up at the dot.
2. Fold under.
3. Bring the ends together.
Turn over and repeat.

27

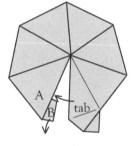

Only the top half is drawn. Tuck
the tab under A. B goes into
the lower half when the same
folds are repeated below.

28

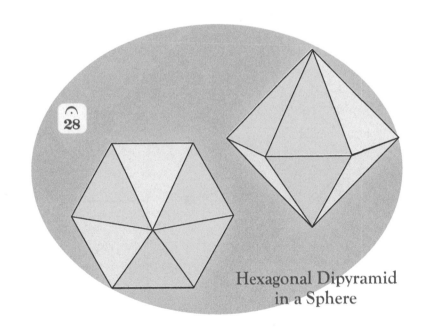

**Hexagonal Dipyramid
in a Sphere**

Jackstone

The jackstone has six points. It is composed of six square pyramids on the faces of a cube. The apex angle on each triangular face is 45°.

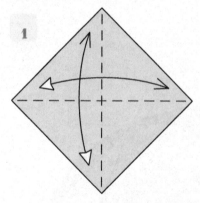

Fold and unfold.

Crease on the left.

Unfold and rotate 180°.

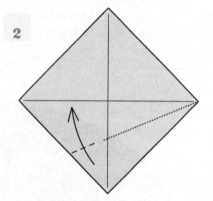

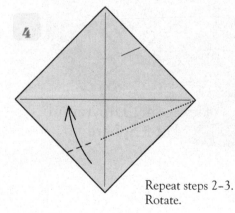

Repeat steps 2–3. Rotate.

Fold and unfold. Rotate 180°.

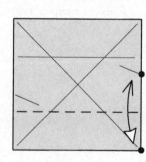

Fold and unfold. Rotate 90°.

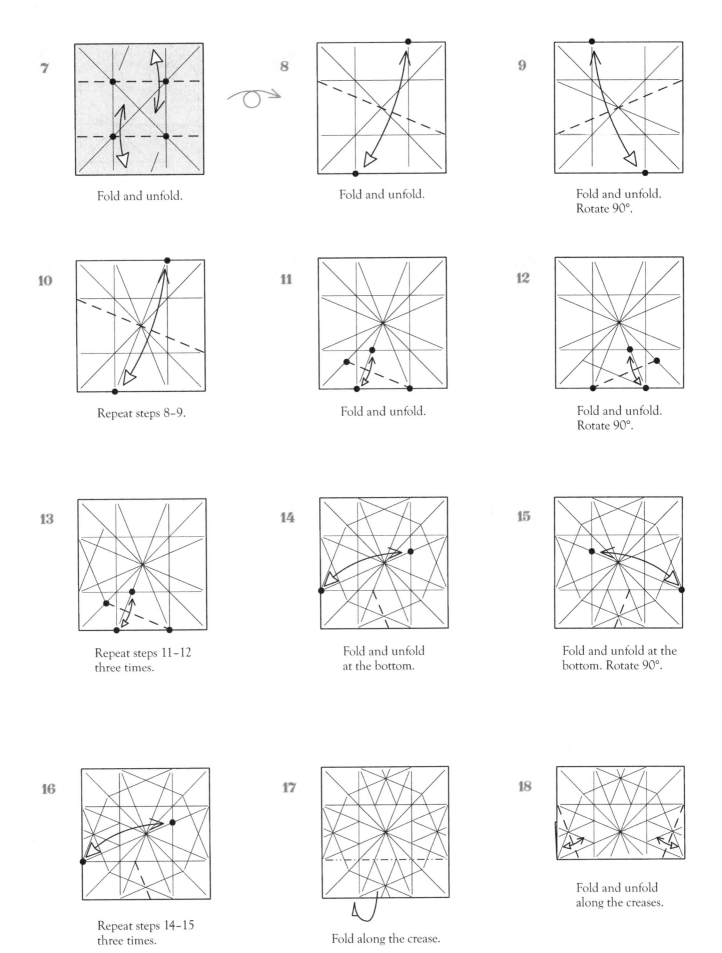

7 Fold and unfold.

8 Fold and unfold.

9 Fold and unfold. Rotate 90°.

10 Repeat steps 8–9.

11 Fold and unfold.

12 Fold and unfold. Rotate 90°.

13 Repeat steps 11–12 three times.

14 Fold and unfold at the bottom.

15 Fold and unfold at the bottom. Rotate 90°.

16 Repeat steps 14–15 three times.

17 Fold along the crease.

18 Fold and unfold along the creases.

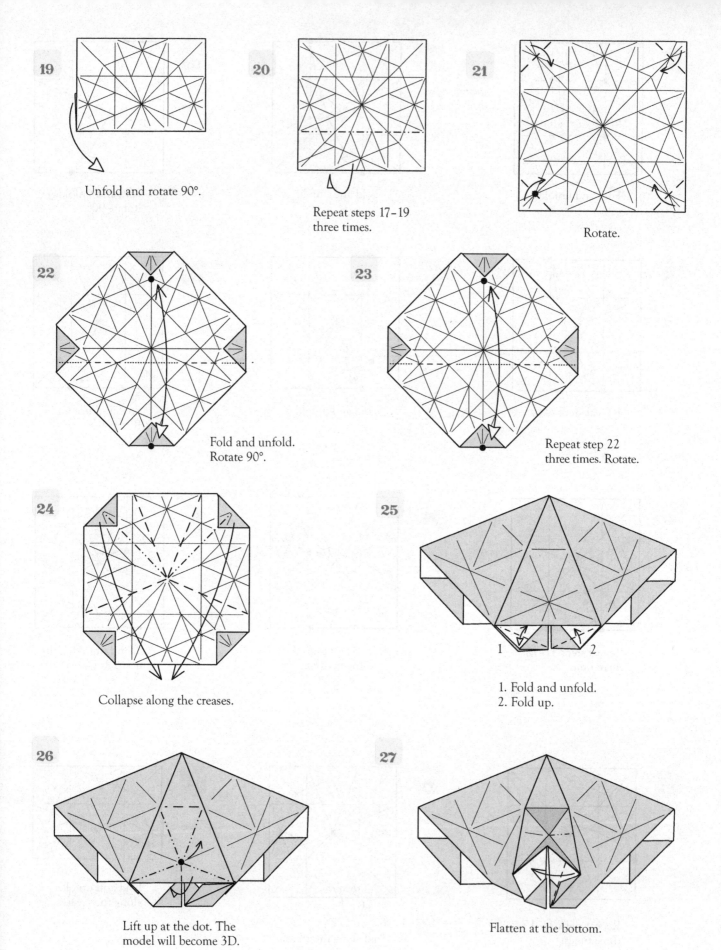

19 Unfold and rotate 90°.

20 Repeat steps 17–19 three times.

21 Rotate.

22 Fold and unfold. Rotate 90°.

23 Repeat step 22 three times. Rotate.

24 Collapse along the creases.

25
1. Fold and unfold.
2. Fold up.

26 Lift up at the dot. The model will become 3D.

27 Flatten at the bottom.

28

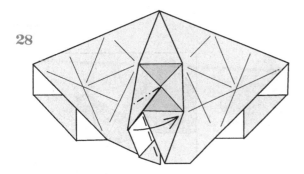

Wrap around and
flatten at the bottom.

29

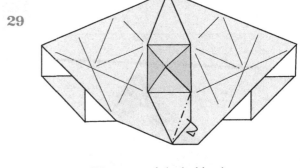

Wrap around the hidden layer.

30

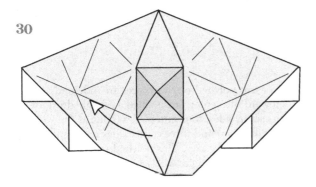

Unfold and rotate 90°.

31

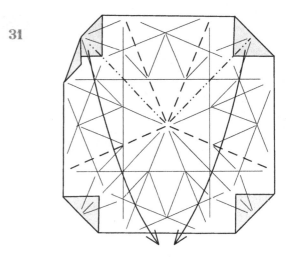

Repeat steps 24–30 on the three
other sides. Do not unfold in
step 30 for the last one.

32

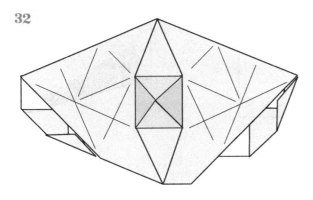

Refold on all the sides. While
assembling the star, the model
will continue to open.

33

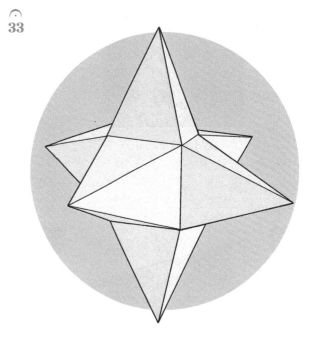

Jackstone

Heptahedron

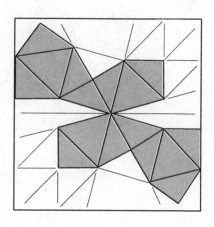

For this polyhedron, four faces are indented toward the center. It is named a heptahedron for its seven sides: four outer sides (same as the octahedron) and three center sides representing the x, y, and z axes. This polyhedron combines equilateral triangles with isosceles right triangles.

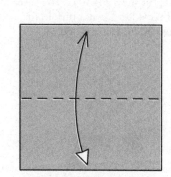

Fold and unfold.

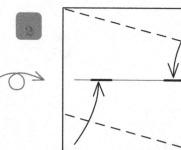

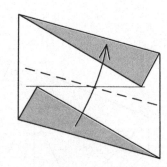

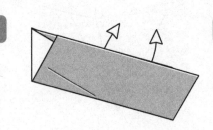

Unfold the two edges.

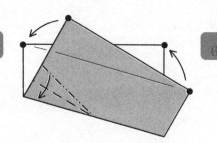

Valley-fold along the crease.
Turn over and repeat.

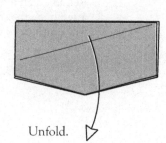

Unfold.

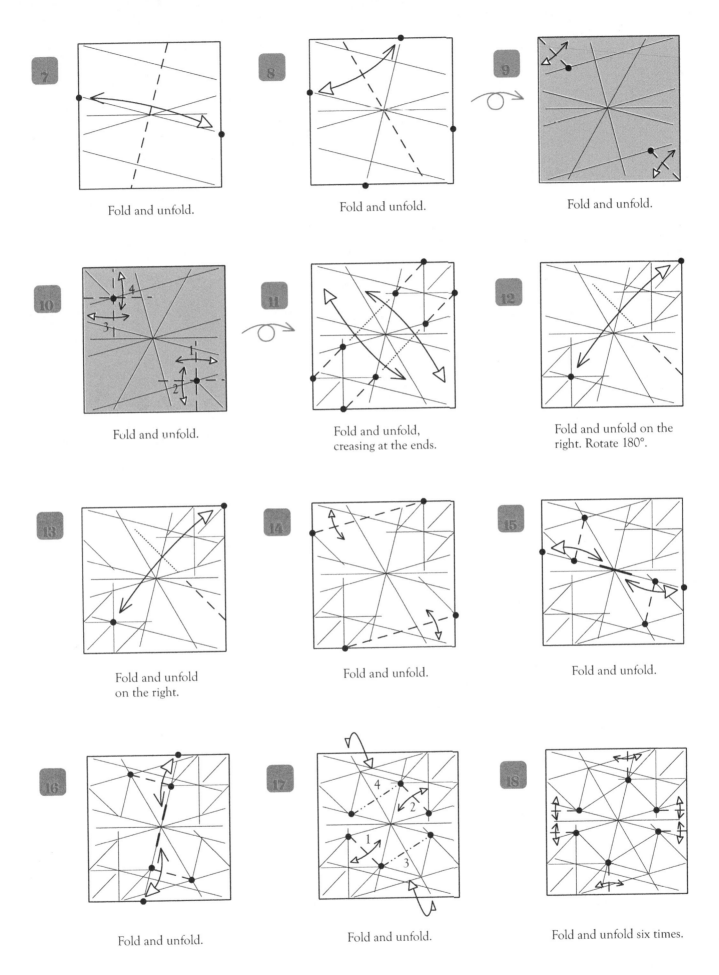

7 Fold and unfold.

8 Fold and unfold.

9 Fold and unfold.

10 Fold and unfold.

11 Fold and unfold, creasing at the ends.

12 Fold and unfold on the right. Rotate 180°.

13 Fold and unfold on the right.

14 Fold and unfold.

15 Fold and unfold.

16 Fold and unfold.

17 Fold and unfold.

18 Fold and unfold six times.

Heptahedron **95**

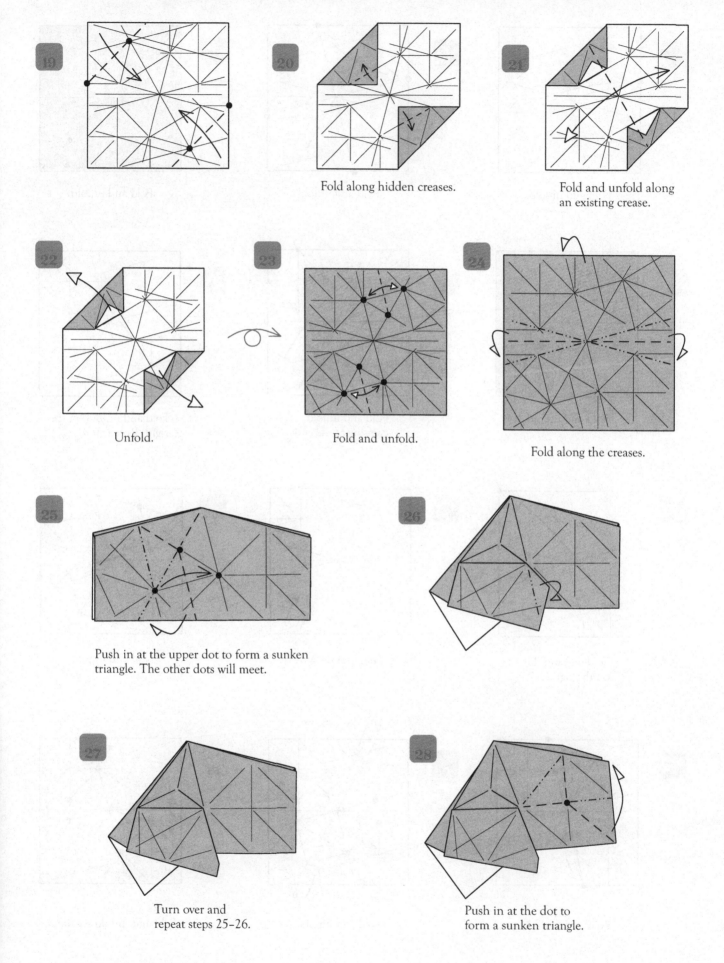

19

20 Fold along hidden creases.

21 Fold and unfold along an existing crease.

22 Unfold.

23 Fold and unfold.

24 Fold along the creases.

25 Push in at the upper dot to form a sunken triangle. The other dots will meet.

26

27 Turn over and repeat steps 25–26.

28 Push in at the dot to form a sunken triangle.

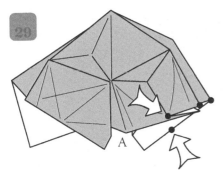

29

Note how some paper comes out at "A". Flatten at the dots so each pair meets.

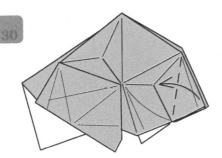

30

Fold all the layers together.

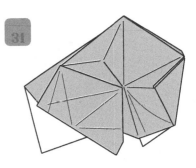

31

Turn over and repeat steps 28–30.

32

Bring the dots together. Rotate.

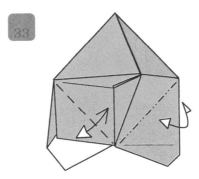

33

Flatten the flaps together. Fold and unfold all the layers.

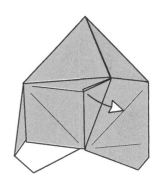

34

Unfold.

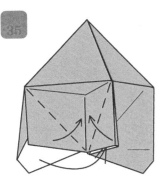

35

Tuck the left flap into the right ones and flatten.

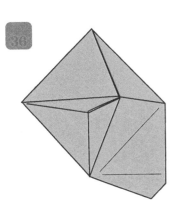

36

Turn over and repeat step 35.

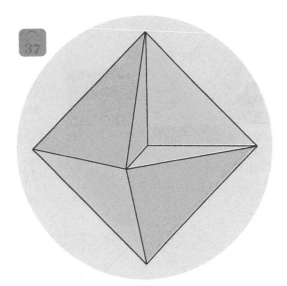

37

Heptahedron

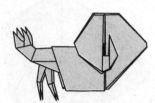

Fourth Movement

Allegro: Melodies Deep in the Ocean

In origami design, sea creatures bring out the zany side, from unusual shapes to lots of legs, tentacles, and other points. The Blue Surgeon, Triggerfish, and Seahorse thrive in the coral reefs. Sailfish and Manta Rays swim in deeper waters. Be careful of the ever-present Jellyfish, though the Leatherback Turtles find them tasty. Squids dart around as they change colors. Hermit Crabs end this origami symphony as they crawl on shore and then swim away.

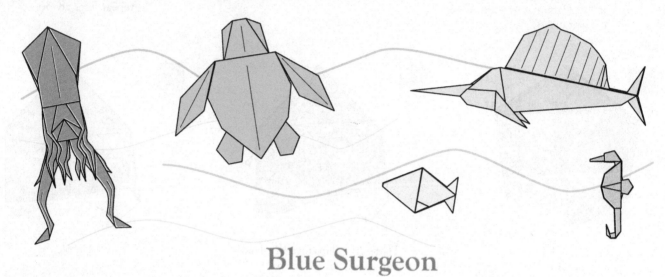

Blue Surgeon

Also called blue surgeon tang or simply blue tang, they appear from light blue to deep purple, depending on their mood. They are an oval shaped flat fish with a body length of 12 inches long. Swimming in large schools in coral reefs, they graze on algae and plankton. The blue surgeon has sharp spines in its tail which contain venom.

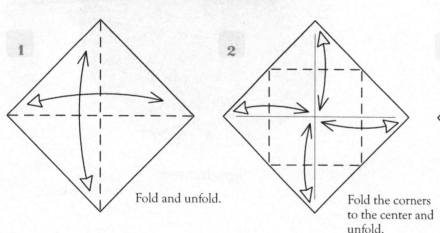

1. Fold and unfold.

2. Fold the corners to the center and unfold.

3. 1. Fold and unfold.
   2. Fold up.

4

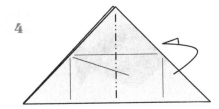

5

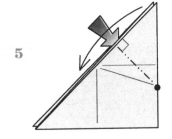

Reverse-fold.

6

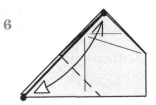

Fold and unfold. Repeat behind and rotate 45°.

7

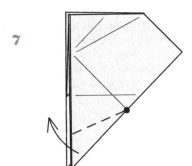

Repeat behind.

8

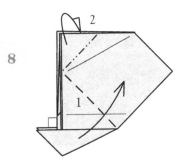

Note the right angle. Fold along the creases at 1 and 2. Repeat behind.

9

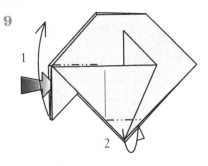

1. Reverse-fold the inner flap.
2. Fold along a partially hidden crease, repeat behind.

10

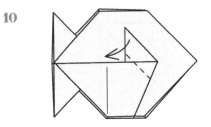

Repeat behind.

11

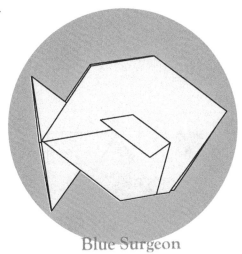

Blue Surgeon

Triggerfish

The triggerfish is an oval shaped fish around 8 to 20 inches long. Swimming in coral reefs, they are colorful, with interesting patterns of spots and stripes. They can swim backward and forward. With strong jaws, they dine on hard invertebrates including crustaceans, mollusks and urchins.

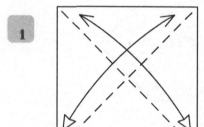

Fold and unfold.

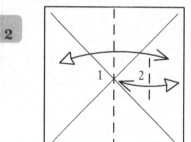

Fold and unfold
at 1 and 2.

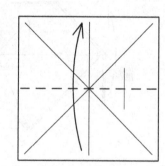

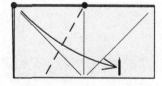

Bring the corner
to the line.

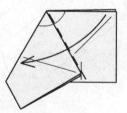

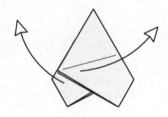

Unfold.

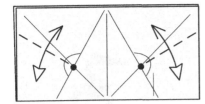

Fold and unfold.

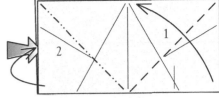

1. Fold along the crease.
2. Reverse-fold.

9

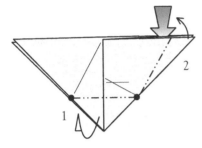

1. Fold behind.
2. Reverse-fold along the crease.

10

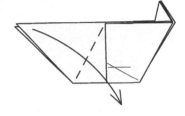

Fold along the crease and repeat behind. Rotate.

11

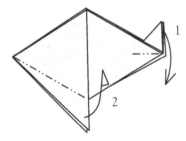

1. Reverse-fold the inner flap.
2. Fold along the crease, repeat behind.

12

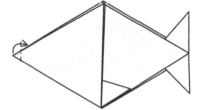

Reverse-fold.

13

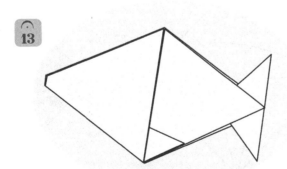

Triggerfish

Seahorse

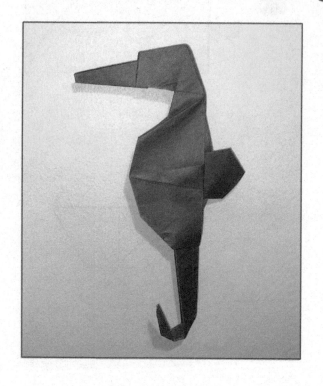

Seahorses are one of the cutest fish. With one small fin in the middle of their back, they are poor swimmers but they can swim up and down. Their tail can wrap around vegetation as they camouflage into the aquatic plants. Hardy eaters, they will eat many meals a day and can consume 3,000 brine shrimp in a day. Instead of fish scales, they have a bony structure which is not tasty to most fish.

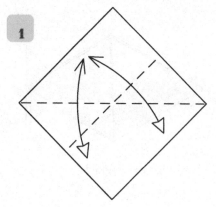

Fold and unfold.

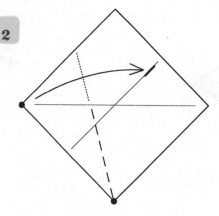

Bring the corner to the line.

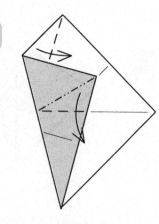

Squash-fold.

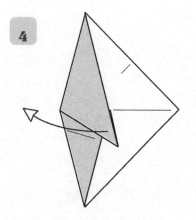

Unfold and rotate 180°.

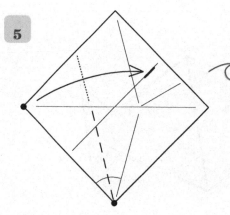

Repeat steps 2–5.

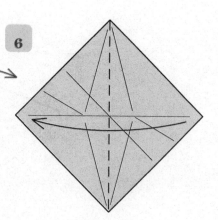

7

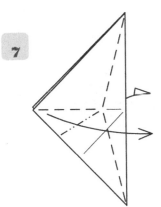

Rabbit-ear along the creases. Repeat behind.

8

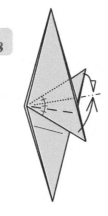

Divide in thirds and repeat behind.

9

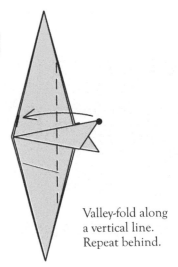

Valley-fold along a vertical line. Repeat behind.

10

Tuck inside and repeat behind.

11

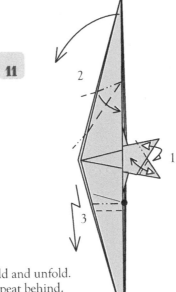

1. Fold and unfold. Repeat behind.
2. Crimp-fold.
3. Crimp-fold.

12

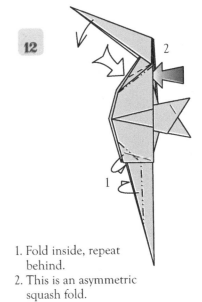

1. Fold inside, repeat behind.
2. This is an asymmetric squash fold.

13

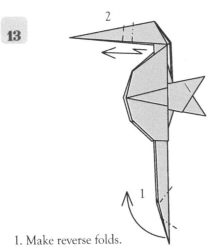

1. Make reverse folds.
2. Crimp-fold.

14

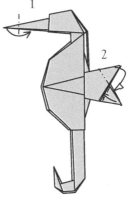

1. Reverse-fold.
2. Tuck inside, repeat behind.

15

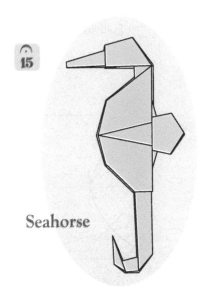

Seahorse

Sailfish

The sailfish is one of the fastest swimming fish. Hunting in groups, they use their large dorsal fins to contain fish. As the top predator in the ocean, they spend most of their time near the surface of the ocean and dive deeper in search of fish, crustaceans, and squid. Their skin color changes to communicate their mood.

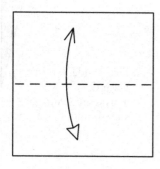

Fold and unfold.

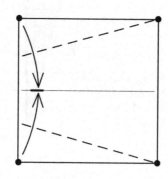

Bring the corners to the line.

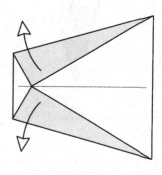

Unfold.

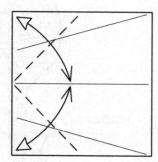

Fold and unfold.

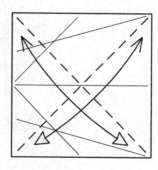

Fold and unfold.

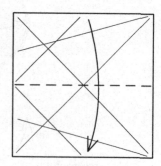

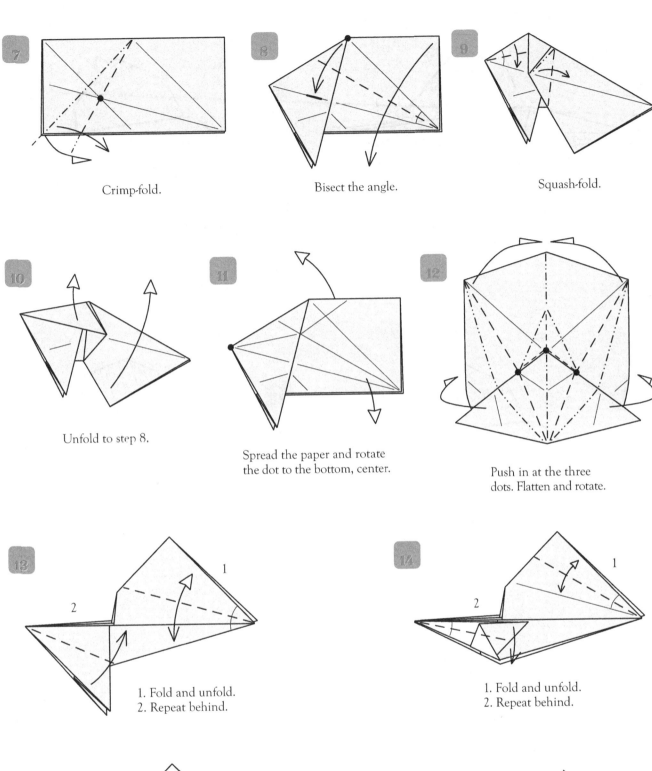

7 Crimp-fold.

8 Bisect the angle.

9 Squash-fold.

10 Unfold to step 8.

11 Spread the paper and rotate the dot to the bottom, center.

12 Push in at the three dots. Flatten and rotate.

13
1
2
1. Fold and unfold.
2. Repeat behind.

14
1
2
1. Fold and unfold.
2. Repeat behind.

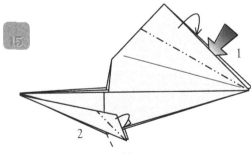

15
1
2
1. Reverse-fold.
2. Reverse-fold, repeat behind.

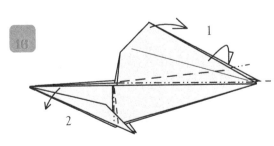

16
1
2
1. Crimp-fold.
2. Crimp-fold.

Sailfish **105**

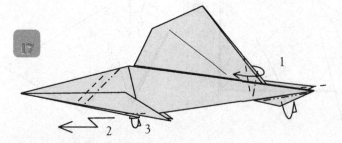

17

1. Repeat behind at the tail.
2. Crimp-fold.
3. Fold inside, repeat behind.

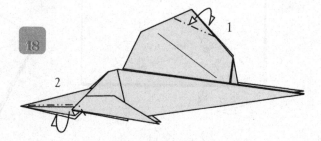

18

1. Fold and unfold.
2. Fold inside, repeat behind.

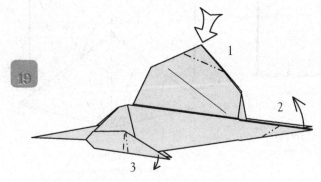

19

1. Sink.
2. Reverse-fold, repeat behind.
3. Pleat-fold, repeat behind.

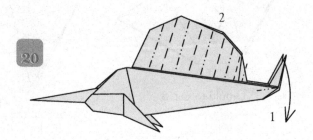

20

1. Reverse-fold.
2. Pleat-fold.

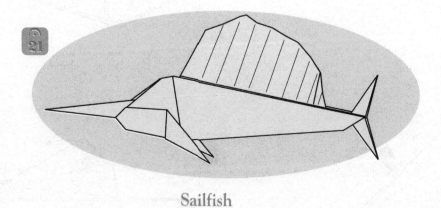

21

Sailfish

Manta Ray

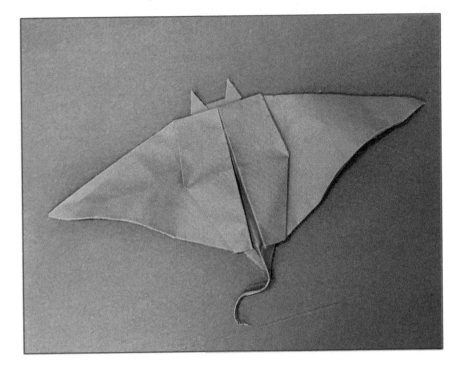

The manta ray is one of the more intelligent fish. Their long term memory gives them a map of a large area and they can pass the mirror test, showing that they can recognize themselves. With a wing span of 26 feet, they leap gracefully out of the water. This gentle fish does not have a stinger in its long tail and feeds on plankton. Swimming in coral reefs, tropical and subtropical waters, they can camouflage into the background.

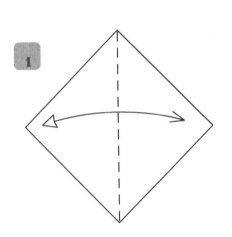

Fold and unfold.

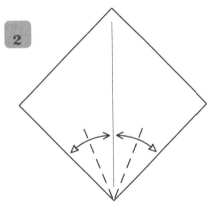

Fold and unfold.

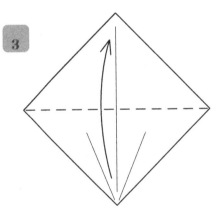

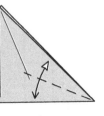

Fold and unfold the top layer.

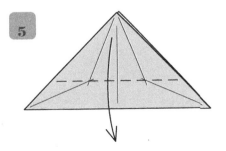

Fold the top layer down.

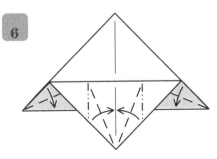

Make squash folds.

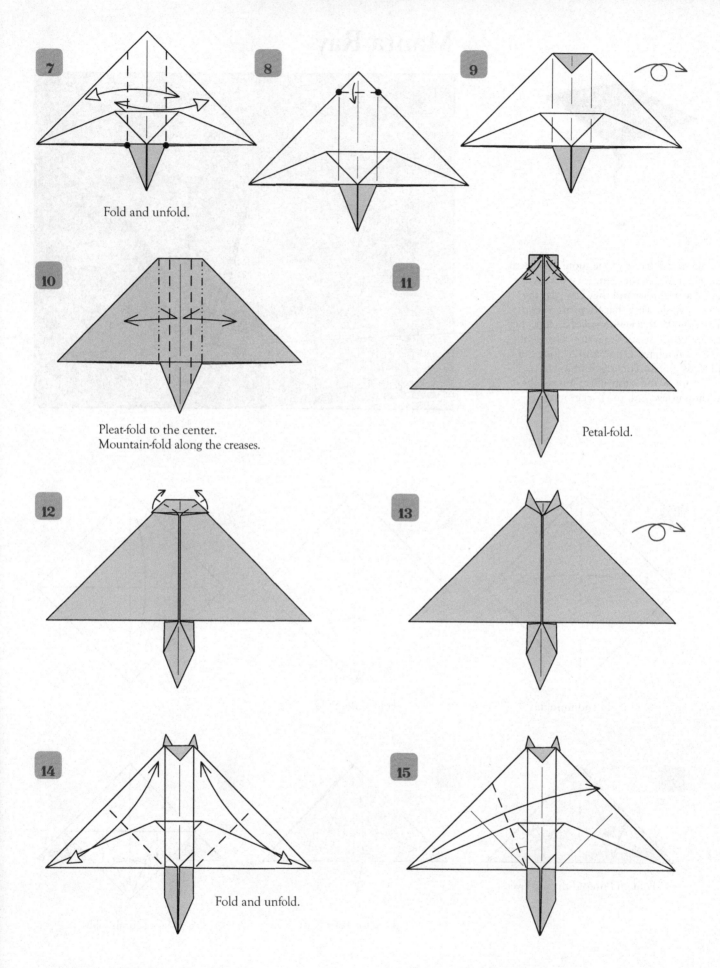

7 Fold and unfold.

8

9

10 Pleat-fold to the center.
Mountain-fold along the creases.

11 Petal-fold.

12

13

14 Fold and unfold.

15

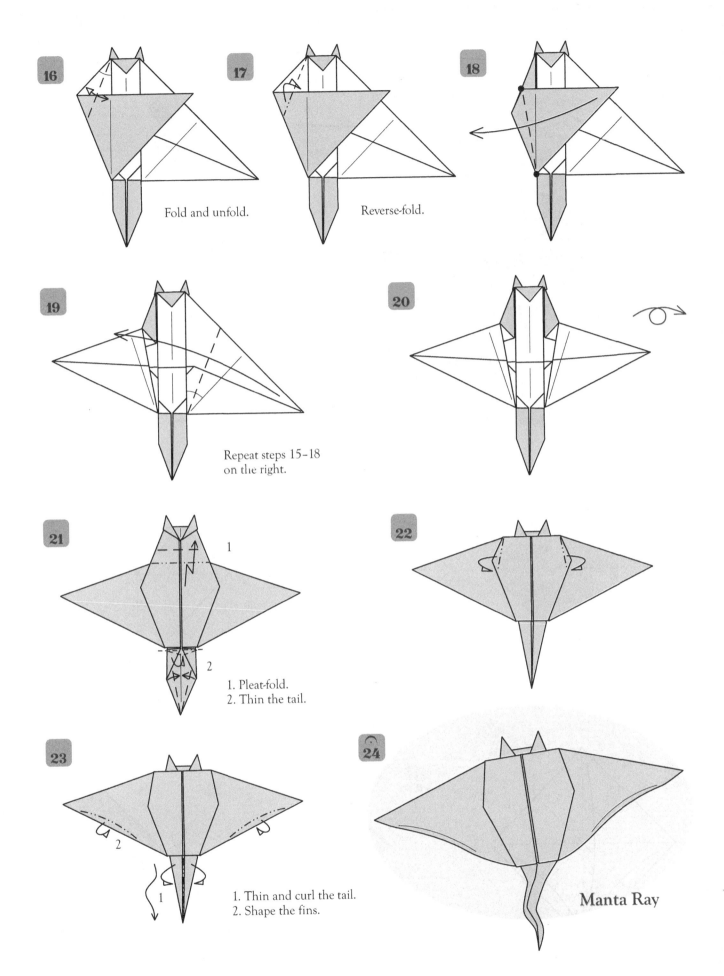

16

Fold and unfold.

17

Reverse-fold.

18

19

Repeat steps 15–18 on the right.

20

21

1. Pleat-fold.
2. Thin the tail.

22

23

1. Thin and curl the tail.
2. Shape the fins.

24

Manta Ray

Jellyfish

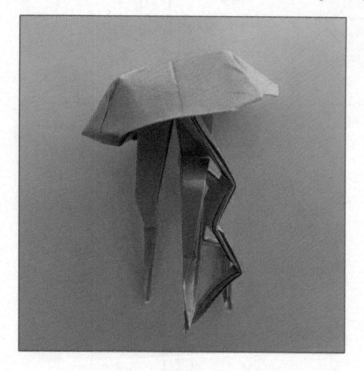

Referred to as "gelatinous zooplankton", jellyfish are invertebrates from the phylum *Cnidaria*. They drift with the current but can move downward. Without a brain, they have nerves to pick up smell, light, gravity, and water motion. As a living ancient animal from over 600 million years ago, they are found in waters all around the world. With stinging tentacles, they are both predator and prey. Jellyfish symbolize beauty and danger.

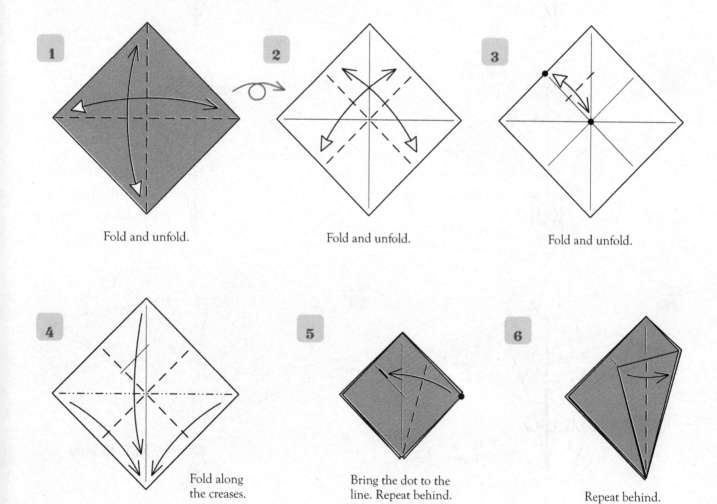

1 Fold and unfold.

2 Fold and unfold.

3 Fold and unfold.

4 Fold along the creases.

5 Bring the dot to the line. Repeat behind.

6 Repeat behind.

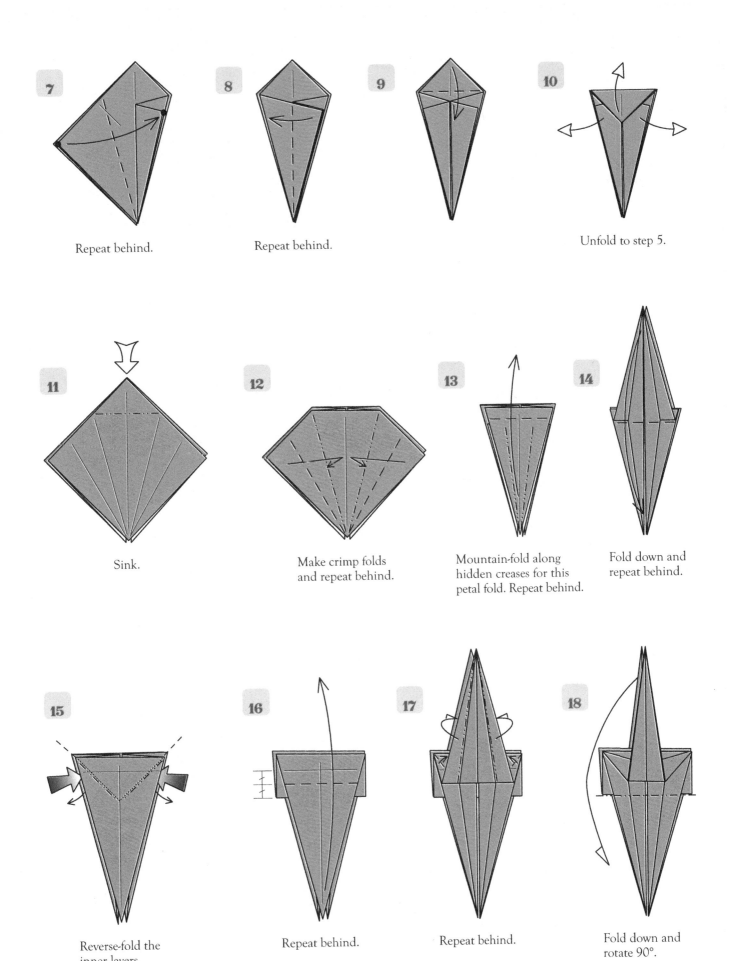

7 Repeat behind.

8 Repeat behind.

9

10 Unfold to step 5.

11 Sink.

12 Make crimp folds and repeat behind.

13 Mountain-fold along hidden creases for this petal fold. Repeat behind.

14 Fold down and repeat behind.

15 Reverse-fold the inner layers.

16 Repeat behind.

17 Repeat behind.

18 Fold down and rotate 90°.

19

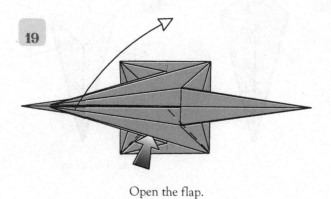

Open the flap.

20

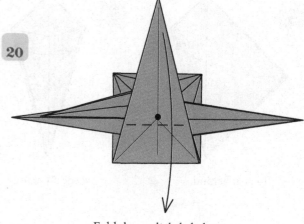

Fold down slightly below
the dot and make some
small squash folds.

21

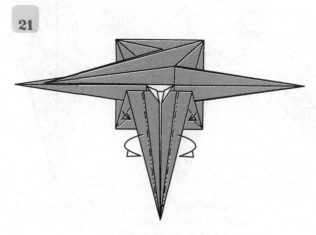

Thin the flap.

22

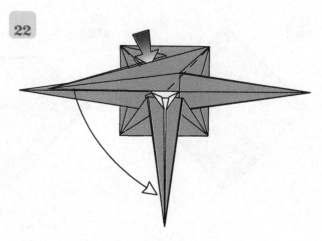

Repeat steps 19–21
on the top.

23

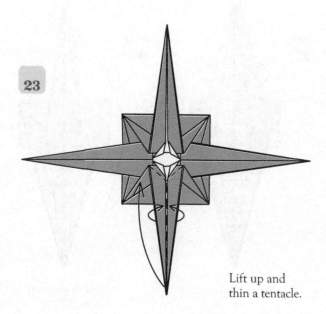

Lift up and
thin a tentacle.

24

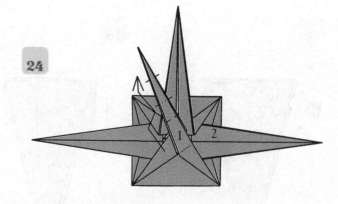

1. Pleat-fold.
2. Repeat steps 23–24 three times
   to form the other tentacles.
Rotate the top to the bottom.

25

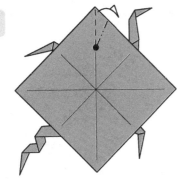

Puff out at the dot.

26

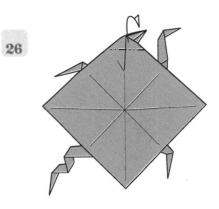

Fold behind
and rotate 90°.

27

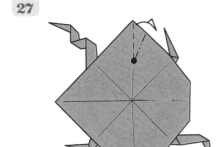

Repeat steps 25–26
three times.

28

Jellyfish

Leatherback Turtle

The leatherback turtle is the largest turtle in the world measuring 4 to 8 feet long and weighing 2,200 pounds. Still the same as they were during the age of dinosaurs, they do not have a hard shell nor scales like other turtles. Instead, they have tough, rubbery skin. Everyday they consume their own body weight in food, dining on jellyfish and sponges. With long front flippers, they swim great distances throughout their lives and can dive 4,000 feet deep, deeper than most marine mammals. Unlike most reptiles, they can maintain a warm body temperature due to size, body fat, and other adaptations.

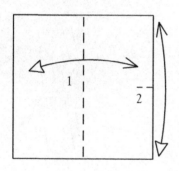

1. Fold and unfold.
2. Fold and unfold on the edge.

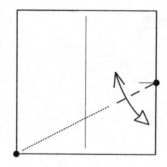

Fold and unfold.

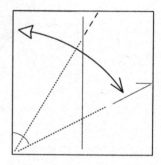

Biesect the angle. Fold and unfold at the top.

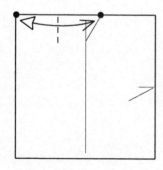

Fold and unfold.

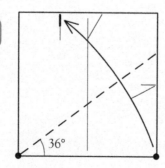

Bring the corner to the line. The angle is exactly 36°.

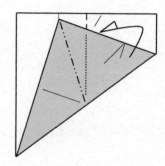

Valley-fold along the crease for this reverse fold.

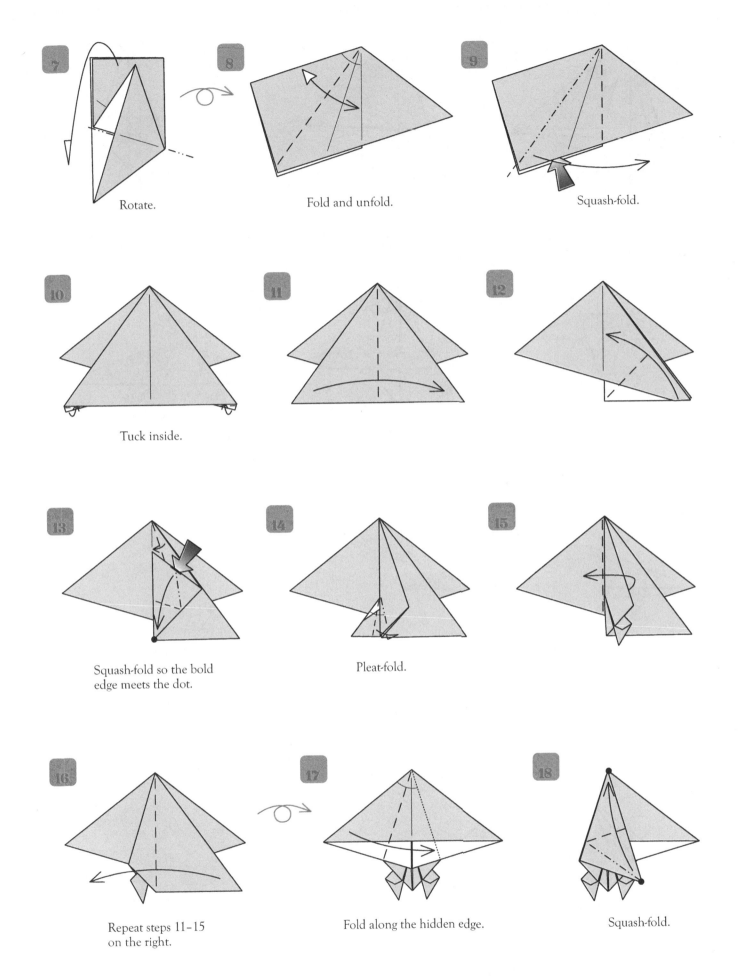

7 Rotate.

8 Fold and unfold.

9 Squash-fold.

10 Tuck inside.

11

12

13 Squash-fold so the bold edge meets the dot.

14 Pleat-fold.

15

16 Repeat steps 11–15 on the right.

17 Fold along the hidden edge.

18 Squash-fold.

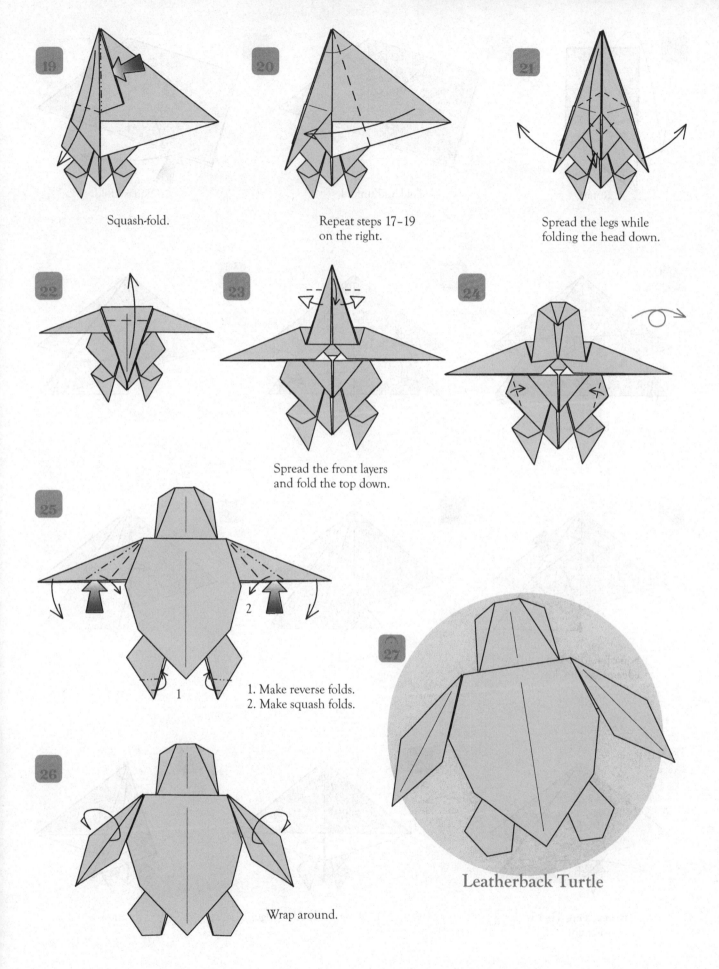

19 Squash-fold.

20 Repeat steps 17–19 on the right.

21 Spread the legs while folding the head down.

22

23 Spread the front layers and fold the top down.

24

25
1. Make reverse folds.
2. Make squash folds.

26 Wrap around.

27 Leatherback Turtle

Squid

With eight legs and two longer tentacles, squid are the fastest swimmers of all the invertebrates. They swim tail-first. The skin has specialized cells to change colors to blend into the surroundings. Deep-sea species glow in the dark. They feed on shrimp and small fish. When threatened, they will squirt a cloud of black ink.

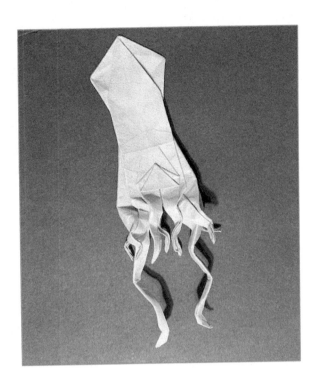

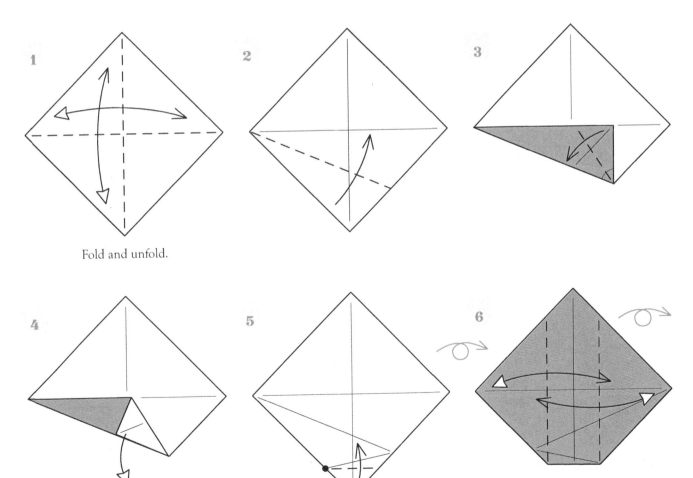

1

Fold and unfold.

2

3

4

Unfold.

5

6

Fold and unfold.

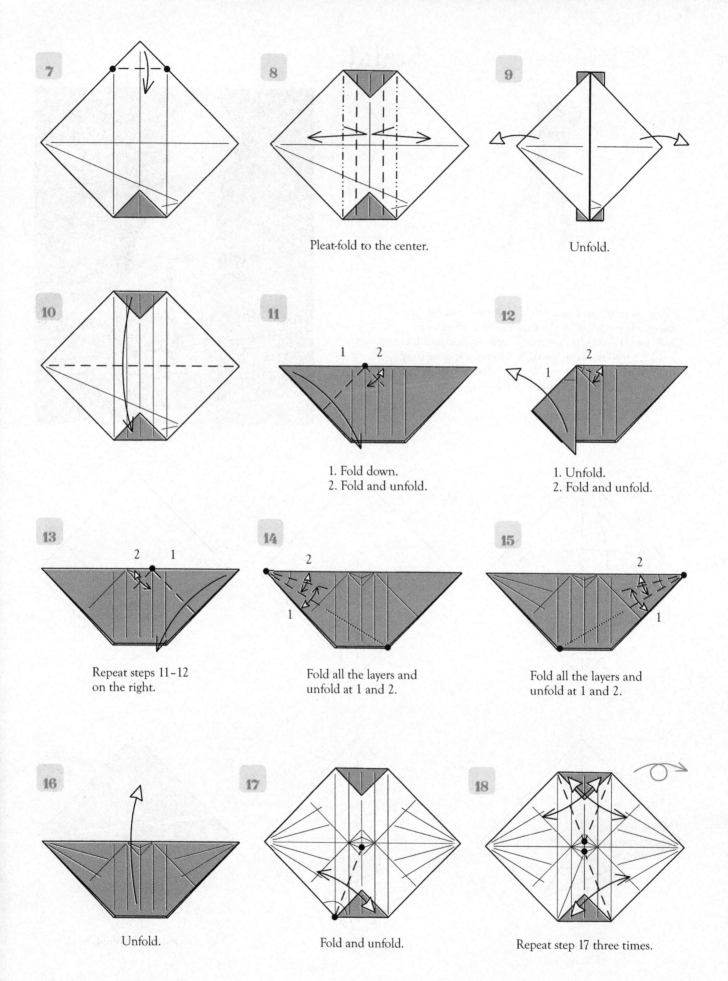

7

8

Pleat-fold to the center.

9

Unfold.

10

11

1. Fold down.
2. Fold and unfold.

12

1. Unfold.
2. Fold and unfold.

13

Repeat steps 11–12
on the right.

14

Fold all the layers and
unfold at 1 and 2.

15

Fold all the layers and
unfold at 1 and 2.

16

Unfold.

17

Fold and unfold.

18

Repeat step 17 three times.

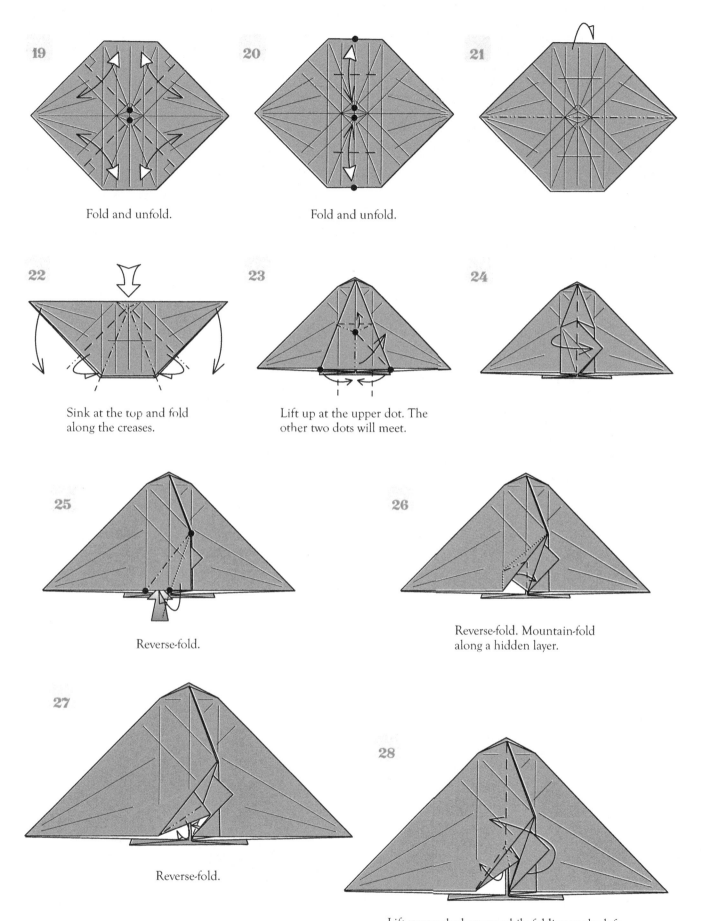

19

Fold and unfold.

20

Fold and unfold.

21

22

Sink at the top and fold along the creases.

23

Lift up at the upper dot. The other two dots will meet.

24

25

Reverse-fold.

26

Reverse-fold. Mountain-fold along a hidden layer.

27

Reverse-fold.

28

Lift up on the bottom while folding to the left.

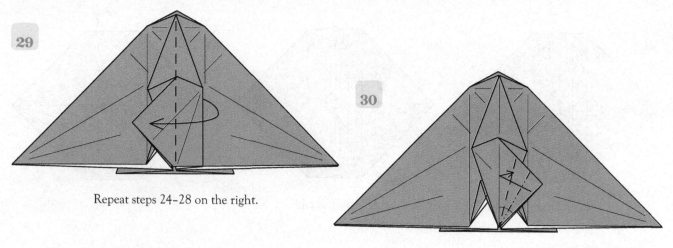

29

Repeat steps 24–28 on the right.

30

Fold in thirds.

31

Unfold.

32

Squash-fold.

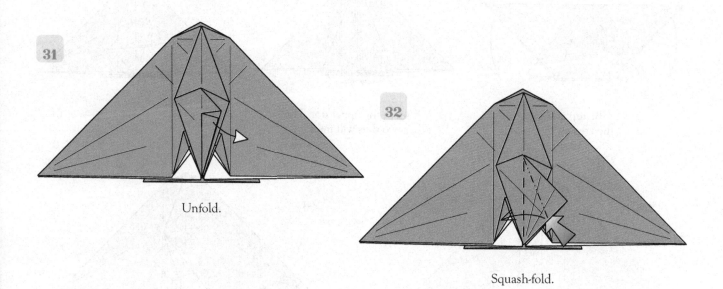

33

This is similar to a petal fold.

34

Squash-fold.

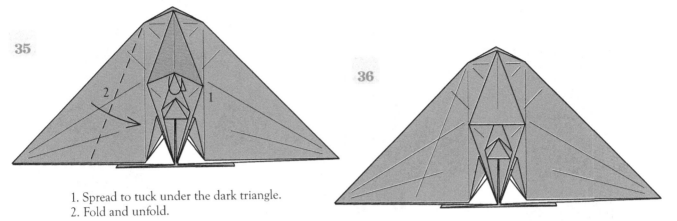

35

1. Spread to tuck under the dark triangle.
2. Fold and unfold.

36

Repeat steps 23–35 behind.

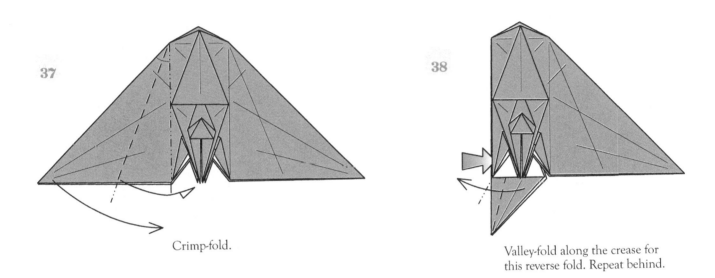

37

Crimp-fold.

38

Valley-fold along the crease for this reverse fold. Repeat behind.

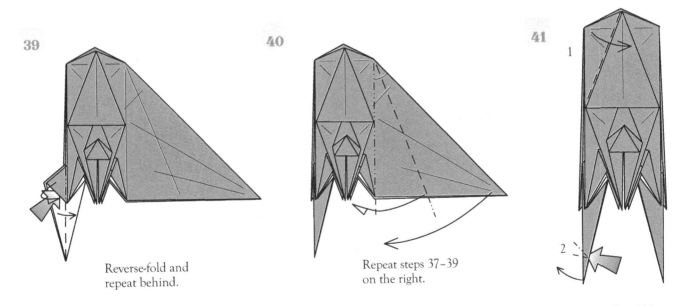

39

Reverse-fold and repeat behind.

40

Repeat steps 37–39 on the right.

41

1. Valley-fold.
2. Crimp-fold.

42

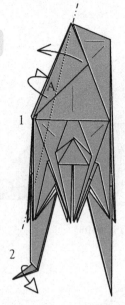

1. Mountain-fold the inner flap so region A is hidden inside.
2. Pull out the top layers, repeat behind.

43

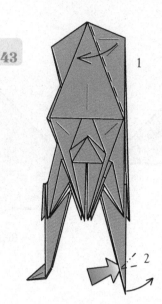

Repeat steps 41–42 on the right.

44

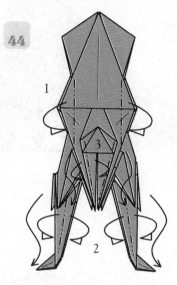

Fold on the left and right.
1. Fold inside, repeat behind.
2. Thin and curl the long tentacles.
3. Thin and curl the central tentacles, repeat behind.

45

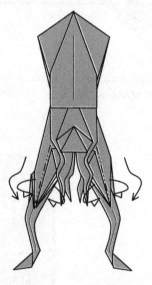

Thin and shape the tentacles, repeat behind.

46

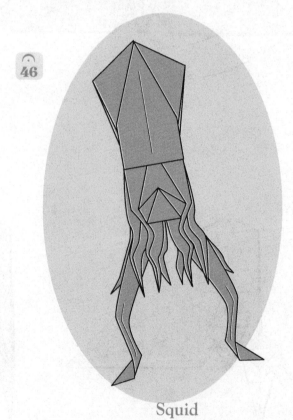

Squid

Hermit Crab

Hermit crabs are found along open shorelines and mud flats. These social crustaceans travel in large groups in search of food and new shells. They feed at night on plankton, small fish and small invertebrates. As they grow, they need to find larger and larger shells. They can breathe on land and communicate by chirping.

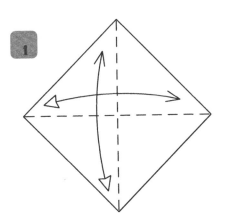

Fold and unfold.

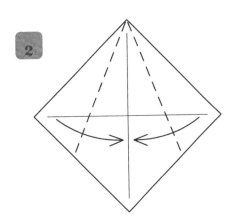

Fold to the center.

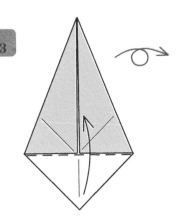

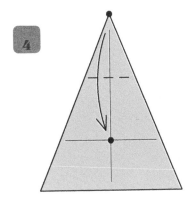

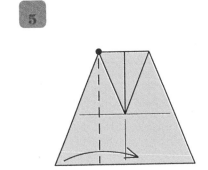

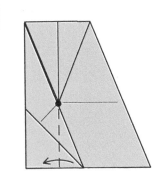

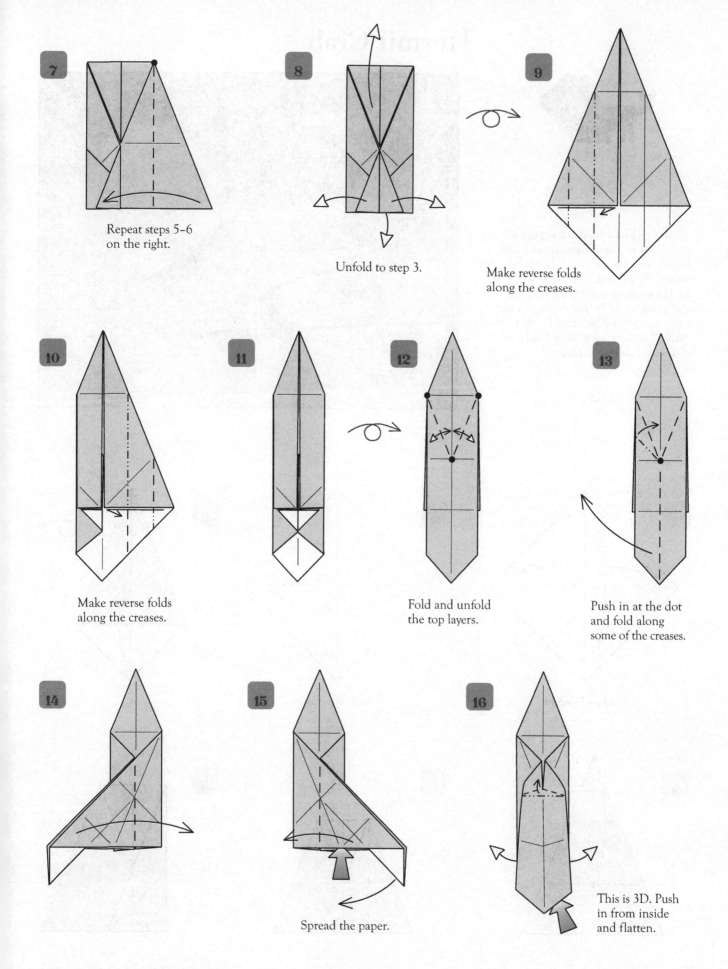

7 Repeat steps 5–6 on the right.

8 Unfold to step 3.

9 Make reverse folds along the creases.

10 Make reverse folds along the creases.

11

12 Fold and unfold the top layers.

13 Push in at the dot and fold along some of the creases.

14

15 Spread the paper.

16 This is 3D. Push in from inside and flatten.

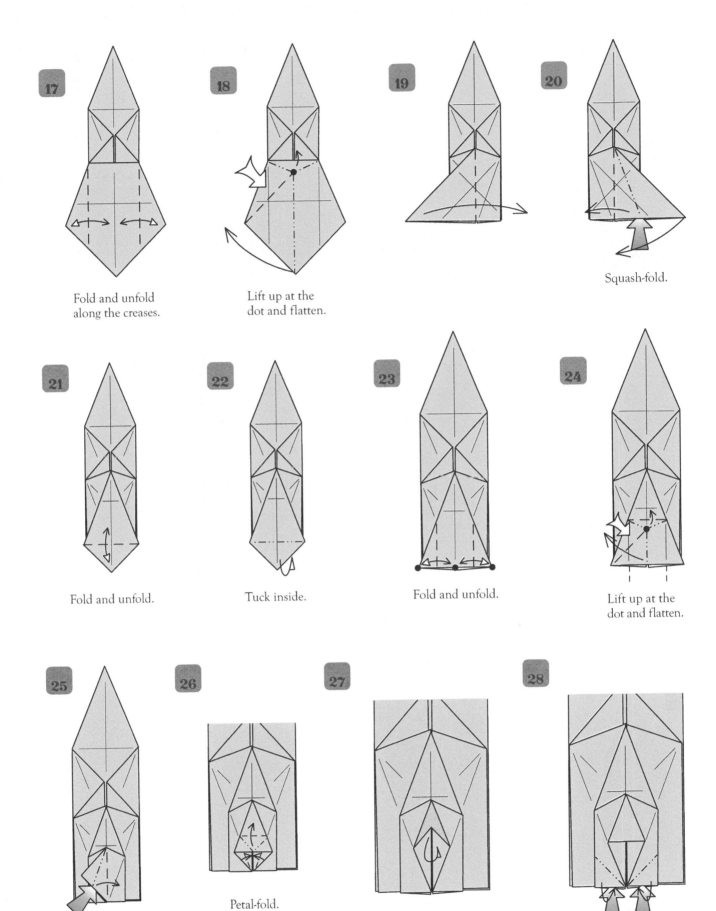

17 Fold and unfold along the creases.

18 Lift up at the dot and flatten.

19

20 Squash-fold.

21 Fold and unfold.

22 Tuck inside.

23 Fold and unfold.

24 Lift up at the dot and flatten.

25 Squash-fold.

26 Petal-fold.

27 Spread to tuck under the dark triangle.

28 Make reverse folds.

Hermit Crab **125**

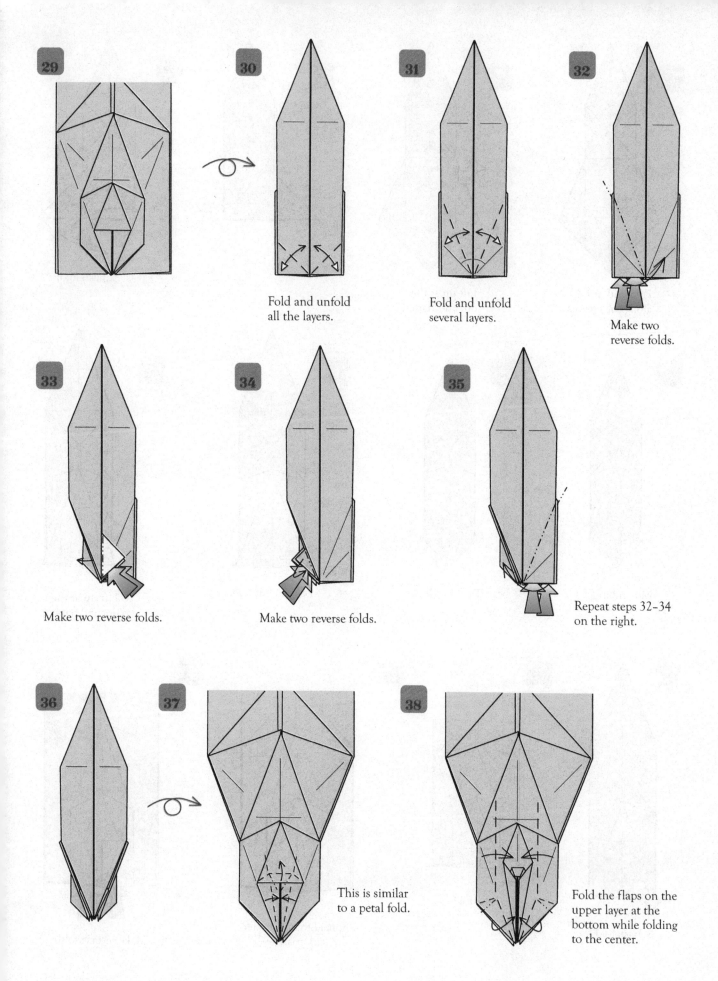

29

30

Fold and unfold
all the layers.

31

Fold and unfold
several layers.

32

Make two
reverse folds.

33

Make two reverse folds.

34

Make two reverse folds.

35

Repeat steps 32–34
on the right.

36

37

This is similar
to a petal fold.

38

Fold the flaps on the
upper layer at the
bottom while folding
to the center.

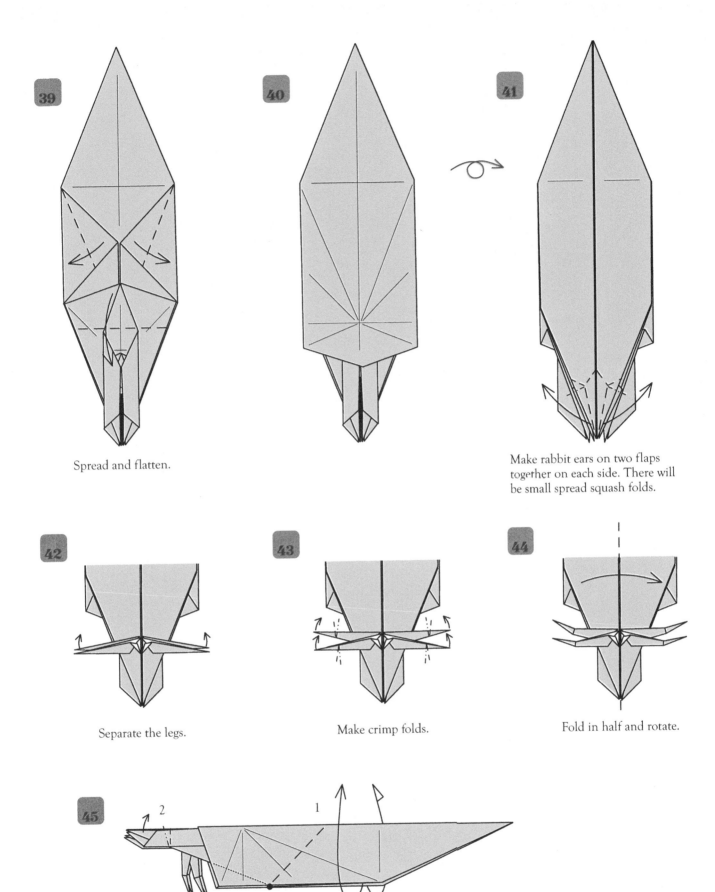

39 Spread and flatten.

40

41 Make rabbit ears on two flaps together on each side. There will be small spread squash folds.

42 Separate the legs.

43 Make crimp folds.

44 Fold in half and rotate.

45
1. Outside-reverse-fold.
2. Pleat-fold, repeat behind.

46

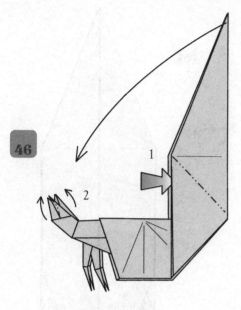

1. Reverse-fold.
2. Spread and shape the claw, repeat behind.

47

Outside-reverse-fold.

48

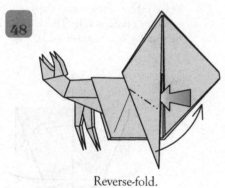

Reverse-fold.

49

1. Outside-reverse-fold.
2. Fold inside, repeat behind.

50

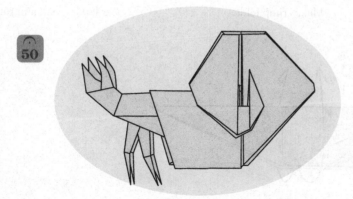

Hermit Crab

Made in the USA
Columbia, SC
10 February 2025

53192503R00072